Create your own sign making business from scratch

Copyright © Phillip J Fenton 2009
All Rights Reserved

No part of this book may be reproduced in any form,
by photocopying or by any electronic or mechanical means,
Including information storage or retrieval systems,
without permission in writing from both the copyright
owner and the publisher of this book

First Published Date - March 2009

ISBN: 978-0-9564434-0-3

The Dream

A man lay on his bed at the end of his life waiting to die.
His dream came to pay his last respects and bid farewell to the man who had never used it.
As it entered the room the man looked down in shame.
"Why did you not realise me ?" the dream asked.
"Because I was afraid," the man said.
"Afraid of what," said the dream.
"I was afraid I would fail."
"But haven't you failed by not attempting to use me?".
"Yes I did, but I always thought there would be tomorrow."
"You Fool!" said the dream "Did it never occur to you that there was only ever today? The moment that you are in right now?
Do you think that now that death is here that you can put it off until tomorrow?".
"No". said the man, a tear gently rolling down his cheek.
The dream was softer now, because it knew that there were two types of pain, the pain of discipline and the pain of regret, and while discipline weighs ounces, regret weighs pounds.
Then the dream leant forward to gently wipe away the tear and said,
" You need only have taken the first step and I would have taken one to meet you, for the only thing that ever separated us was the belief in your mind that you couldn't have me".
Then they said goodbye and they both died.

Mark Baker 2000

Foreword

This book was deliberately written with the beginner in mind. It is the sort of guide I wish I could have read when I first began to investigate sign making as a business opportunity. Accordingly, it goes back to the very basics and assumes the reader has no prior knowledge of the modern day methods used in signmaking.

Beginning with descriptions of the processes and materials used, it then leads the reader through the learning steps required to allow him or her to understand the fundamentals required to set up and run a small vinyl based signmaking company.

It is difficult to condense into a single book all of the information and knowledge required, but hopefully, there is sufficient starter information available to allow the reader to begin to move forward and ask the right questions to learn enough to allow him or her to establish their own successful venture.

Phill Fenton – March 2009

CONTENTS

Introduction
About this book

Section 1 - Overview
A description of the business – its attraction and possibilities

Section 2 - Basic Equipment required
An overview of the type of equipment you will need to run your business

Section 3 – Building a workbench
How to build a rugged and durable work bench

Section 4 – Sign Software Required
Description of the difference between Vector Drawn and Rendered images and the types of software you will need.

Section 5 - Substrates
Description of the various materials used to make signs

Section 6 - Vinyls and Cutting Basics
How to cut and weed vinyl, and a description of vinyl types

Section 7 - Vinyl application techniques
Description of the two main methods of applying vinyl. Dry versus wet – the advantages and disadvantages of each

Section 8 - Working with multiple colours
How to produce signs made up from more than one colour of vinyl

Section 9 - Fitting signs using Sign Trim
How to manufacture a sign frame and use this to fit sign panels to a building

Section 10 - Vehicle signs
How to go about designing and applying vehicle signs

Section 11 - Flat cut lettering signs
How to design, produce and fit flat cut lettering

Section 12 - Basic principles of good sign layout

A lesson in good design based on the teachings of Mike Stevens

Section 13 - How to price your work

What to consider when determining your pricing structure, and common methods used to price signs

Section 14 - Marketing your business

How to go about getting your customers

Section 15 – Premises

Pros and cons of working from home, from a shop, or from an industrial unit

Section 16 – The internet and its impact on sign making

How the internet has influenced and assisted the sign business

Section 17– Your Business Plan

A template for your business plan

Conclusion

Index

Introduction

I have spent the last 13 years (along with my wife Alison) earning a living as a full time sign maker. When we set up in 1996 we had no prior experience in the sign industry, but I had a very strong desire to run my own business having spent the previous 20 years of my life as an employee in a large brewing organisation. At that time Alison was in the middle of a career break having given up work to bring up our two young children. She was at the stage of considering a return to work but did not relish the thought of returning to her old career in banking. I was also disillusioned with my current career and persuaded Alison that we should start our own business and become masters of our own destiny.

Back in 1995/6, having examined various business ideas we came to the conclusion that a small sign manufacturing business was the ideal opportunity for us. I was attracted by the creative side of sign making, and even though (at that time) I had never made a sign before, I could at least visualise myself running this type of business. (I'm a great believer that if you can imagine yourself doing something, then you've a good chance of achieving that aim).

Before we started, I had already had a good deal of experience using PCs in my existing occupation, and I believed that if I could master the software used in sign design and cutting, then I was halfway there!

Of course, there is much more to running a successful sign business than learning how to use sign design software and a vinyl cutter, but I didn't realise this at the time.

Since we started, I have also become an occasional guest speaker at small business gateway seminars held in Edinburgh and Livingston. These are government funded seminars designed to encourage and help individuals to start up their own businesses of all types. At these seminars I speak about my experiences in setting up our sign company. www.bgateway.com

The biggest single mistake I think we made in the early days was to under value our work. Pricing is an area that I believe causes most concern to many new companies. So, for that reason I will be devoting a full chapter discussing pricing at a later stage in this book.

Under pricing your work not only affects your business, it affects your competitors too because it creates an expectation of "cheaper prices" for the customer making it harder for everyone in the industry to run a viable and sustainable operation.

So why am I writing this? – My reason is simply in order to help new starts to get into the industry and to encourage them to do it properly.

My belief is there are too many people just dabbling in this type of business, doing it part time or as a hobby. Many would like to take it more seriously but are perhaps unsure as to how to progress beyond "hobby" or part time work. I believe that there will always be new people attracted to and moving into the industry, thus creating greater competition for ourselves and others. There is nothing we can do to prevent this. So rather than resist it, I believe the best course of action is to encourage newcomers in the belief that we actually all share the same long term needs (i.e. to run a viable and sustainable business). I also believe it is better to share knowledge for the overall betterment of the industry.

I am very proud of the work we do and the services and products we provide. For that reason, I would prefer to see it full of dedicated people that are busy producing the best work they are capable of.

I have also been inspired by many of the other professional sign manufacturers that I have come across during my time as a sign maker.

Rob Lambie, who established www.uksignboards.com has succeeded in creating one of the most popular on line communities for signmakers today.

Mike Brown (www.mikethesign.com) is probably the most talented vinyl sign maker I have come across. He has taken computer cut vinyl to its very limit which has inspired myself and many others to strive to produce better work.

If I can encourage in others, some of the values I have learned from certain individuals, then I believe I have achieved something of real value which is beyond monetary measurement.

The late Mike Stevens (Author of "Mastering Layout") said:-

"Always look back, and always look forward. Improve your skills and product at every opportunity. You'll not only be protecting your future, but you'll be helping to create a better market for all sign makers. There is a natural phenomenon that takes place in a healthy economy – and that is that the more good sign makers there are, the greater the interest and demand there is for the product. In the final analysis we are in this together. Let's keep the lines of communication open and intellectually honest, and the standards high!"

Section 1 – Overview

So why would anyone want to start a sign business?

For me it was to be self employed and independent. There is nothing more satisfying than working for yourself. Believe me! I worked for 20 years in a large organisation and the satisfaction I get now from working for myself does not come close to comparing to the job satisfaction I had in my previous career.

My attitude is - you only get one life – this is not a dress rehearsal, this is the real thing. I didn't want to look back in 20 years time and say "what if"?

So that is why I gave up my previous career and became a sign maker (If you try but fail, then surely it is better than to have never tried at all - at least that's my philosophy).

What is your motivation?

Mine was to set up my own company and earn an income that supported me and my family. I originally planned to employ others to do the practical aspect of designing and making signs but soon discovered that this was the area of the business I enjoyed most. Sign making is very creative and consequently is a very satisfying way to earn a living. Since first establishing our business I have modified my ambitions of being an employer/manager to becoming what I would like to believe is a "craftsman". I really do enjoy the creative aspect of what I now do. (This was a very fortunate spin off from my original goal of starting a business that would provide an income for my family).

I always get a great deal of satisfaction from transforming an ordinary van into a mobile advertisement for my clients. And the response I get from customers who are pleased with the work I do tells me it's all worth while. There is nothing I enjoy more than driving about my locality and spotting some of the vehicles I have signed. I can honestly think of no more satisfying an occupation.

What other reasons are there to run your own sign company?

To get rich? – Maybe? - But this would be no easier than in any other trade or profession where you are in competition with other similar traders. Sign businesses can range in size from a simple one man operation working from home to a national company with branches in just about every town and city in the country. The potential is there for someone who is driven enough to build a large sign manufacturing company that could be worth a fortune. The less driven person may simply be content to establish a small business that provided an income doing something that he or she enjoyed doing.

As an example, and as inspiration to others, it is worth noting that in 2008 one of the BSGA (British Signs and Graphics Association) awards for Sign Business of the year went to Astsigns, a company that was first established in 2002/3 as a three man operation. By 2008 (in the space of only six years) the fledgling sign company had grown to a business that employed 27 people with a turnover of 1.8 Million Pounds.

What skills are required?

The skills required cover a huge range - the one man business needs to master all these to some degree in order to run a successful trade. For someone who prefers to "manage" their business, people with the necessary skills can be hired.

On the manufacturing side – the skills required are as follows:

Design Skills – These can be learned. Good design is not an art but is a skill that can be taught. At this stage I would recommend that the book "Mastering Layout" by Mike Stevens be bought and studied. This publication sets out the basic principle of good design and is a must for any serious signmaker. Included later in this book is a guide to understanding the "Natural Layout" skills taught by Mike Stevens.

Software skills – Again these can be learned. There are a number of good drawing packages available for sign designers but mastering any piece of design software takes time to learn.

Computer Skills – The modern sign shop is now so dependant on computers that any owner must have basic computer knowledge to be able to maintain their business. At the very least you need to be able to back up your work on a regular basis in order to get yourself up and running again should you lose your main computer at any time.

A sign maker needs to be reasonably competent at basic handiwork. Sign making involves many different practical skills such as applying vinyl, manufacturing frames. Using a whole range of cutting tools such as table saws, mitre saws, routers and craft knifes. If you also intend to install signs you need the ability to drill and fit signs to buildings as well as install posts in the ground for free standing signs.

What training can you get?

Many sign makers are self taught. It's probably true to say that any competent DIY'er could produce a sign. Only those that are dedicated and keen to learn go on to master the principles of good design that ensures they end up producing excellent work. Unfortunately (or fortunately for some) many customers may not be too discerning and make their buying decisions based on price alone. Therefore if you are the cheapest in your area, you may still get the work no matter how poor your design skills. However, this is hardly a good recipe for establishing a long term business with integrity.

There are a number of colleges offering sign related courses. Before we started our business we attended a night class at Edinburgh Telford College and were taught the basic principles of good sign design as well as the basics of vinyl cutting. Later, once the business was actually trading, my wife Alison and an early employee of ours both then went on to attend an HNC day release course at Edinburghs Telford College. I owe a great deal of thanks to Alex Taylor (one of the lecturers) who encouraged us at the very beginning.

Marketing Skills

An essential skill for any business owner is the ability to market their products and services. In many cases this may involve cold calling which some may find difficult. It's not enough to simply place a few adverts in order to find work. Marketing is a key concern when establishing your business and this will be covered in great detail later where I will describe the many methods and ideas you can use to promote your company.

Small Business Gateway

In Scotland we have Small Business Gateway which offers free advice and courses to provide you with the help and knowledge you need to set up your venture. This is entirely government funded and is well worth investigating. Contact your local small business gateway for free advice or go to www.bgateway.com

People Skills

For the owner manager it is necessary to have a number of people skills. You need to be able to motivate and manage the people you employ. As a representative of your company you also need to have the people skills to relate to your customers.

Legal requirements

Insurance

You must have some insurance in place to cover yourself if things go wrong. As a minimum you will require some indemnity insurance to cover such things as public liability. If working from commercial premises you will need to ensure this is insured (either through your landlord – or if you are the owner – yourself). If working from home you should also check with your home insurance.

You should also consider taking out insurance to cover yourself to drive your customers vehicle. I have a policy that ensures I am covered for any of my customers vehicles under my custody or control. This means I am covered to drive customers vehicles as well as ensuring they are insured whilst stored at my premises.

As with all insurance it is best to seek advice from a professional such as an insurance broker.

Your company format

You will need to make a decision about your trading format. There are a number of options available to you. Each option has it's own advantages and disadvantages. There is no ideal solution that would suit everyone as it is down to personal choices and preferences as well as to an extent being dictated by the type of business you are setting up.

Sole Trader

This is the simplest trading format to use. In effect you need not do anything to trade this way, merely complete a self assessment tax return at the end of each year. The downside to being a sole trader is that you alone will be responsible for any liability that your business incurs.

Partnership

A partnership is very similar to a sole trader except there will be more than one person liable for the business. Each partner will need to complete his or her own tax returns each year. In most partnerships it is usual to draw up a formal agreement between partners in the event of a fall out at a later date. A written agreement at the outset will avoid any complications later should the partnership be dissolved at some point in the future.

Limited company

For many people, a limited liability company is the preferred trading format. By setting up a limited company, the directors are able to minimise their personal exposure to the risk of any liability. The company is recognised as an entity in itself and is responsible for any bad debt. If you are planning to employ others then it is well worth considering going down this route to protect yourself from any possibility of being sued (by a disgruntled ex employee for example). However, being limited does not always mean the directors are immune from any liability. Often when companies require financing, the directors will need to act as guarantors for any loans taken out.

Equally, where criminal negligence is involved, the directors of a company that have acted irresponsibly can still be held to account.

Limited companies require additional accountancy procedures and annual returns must be made to companies house each year.

Limited Liability Partnership

In recent years a new format has been introduced called limited liability partnerships (LLP). This allows a business trading as a partnership to enjoy the same type of limited liability as that offered by a limited company. LLP's were introduced to allow firms of solicitors partnerships (who are not allowed to trade as limited companies) to minimise the individual partners exposure to risk .

Additional accountancy procedures are required when trading as an LLP rather than a simple partnership.

VAT Registration

In Britain, if the value of your taxable supplies in the past 12 months or less has exceeded the current VAT registration threshold of £67,000 (correct at time of writing - February 2009), or if the value of your taxable supplies in the next 30 days alone is expected to exceed this threshold, you must register for VAT.

If your turnover is expected to remain below this threshold, you do not have to register. However, you can still elect to register if you wish to do so.

There are advantages and disadvantages in being VAT registered.

Advantages

You can claim back all the VAT duty paid on all expenses incurred by your business. This includes the cost of equipment bought when setting up. You may also gain some credibility in the eyes of your customers (as not being registered tells your customer that you have a turnover of less than £67,000).

All your VAT registered customers will also be claiming back the duty you charge them – so the fact that your VAT inclusive price may be more than any non registered competitors price will make no difference to your customer.

Disadvantages

When selling to non VAT registered customers they will be paying 15% more than they would have done if you weren't registered. There is also a degree of extra administration required to run your business calculating VAT tax returns each quarter.

If your main customers are predominately the general public, and you expect your turnover to remain below £67,000 a year, then you may benefit by not being registered.

However, my own opinion is that sign making is predominately a "business to business" service and consequently most customers tend to be VAT registered. Thus it makes more sense to become VAT registered at the outset (even if below the threshold that requires you to register anyway).

There are two different ways in which you can choose to have your VAT liability calculated.

The first is based on the difference between the VAT you charge on your products and services, and the VAT you have to pay on products and services your business buys in.

The second is called the flat rate scheme

Providing you do not have a turnover above 150,000 you can elect to pay your VAT as a percentage of your total turnover. This varies from industry to industry - but for signmakers it currently stands at 7.5% (correct at time of writing – Feb 2009) of turnover including VAT. The flat rate scheme is easier to administer and you may end up paying less tax using this method than using the more traditional method.

You should also ensure you use the cash accounting scheme as this ensures you only pay the VAT on invoices that have been paid and ignores invoices raised that are still awaiting payment (until they too have been paid).

As with all things new when setting up in business, everyones circumstances are different. I therefore suggest you contact an accountant and seek professional advice before deciding on what best suits your own needs.

Section 2 - Basic Equipment required

There are a few basic tools and pieces of equipment that are needed to set up a small signmaking business.

Essential Equipment

Vinyl Cutter - For cutting Vinyl

This is the key element in all vinyl sign making systems. The vinyl cutter is the machine that actually produces cut vinyl. There are a huge range of cutters available from companies such as Graphtec, Roland, and Summa to name a few. A good quality cutter will pay for itself many times over and will provide years of reliable service.

Computer – For sign design and driving the vinyl cutter.

Although Apple Macs are very popular amongst designers, in practice the majority of signshops tend to use PCs.

There is no need to spend a fortune on a state of the art high specification machine if your main focus will be in computer cut vinyl.

Vector drawn graphics are not memory hungry and the files produced are very efficient compact files. A well specified budget PC is more than capable of handling the majority of work that the typical vinyl signshop will be producing. Only if you branch into digital printing and design will you need to be thinking about using a more powerful computer.

Sign design and cutting software

You will need a vector drawing package such as a general desk top publishing program like Corel Draw, Adobe Illustrator, or one of many dedicated sign shop software packages that are specifically designed for the sign maker. Typical examples include Signlab, Vinyl master Pro and Easy Sign to name but a few.

Scanner – For Scanning images

A reasonably cheap scanner is all that is required.

Desktop Printer – For printing out designs and quotations to send to customers. Best low cost option is a budget inkjet. Also worth considering is an all in one desktop scanner/printer/photocopier. You can get a reasonable example for well under £100 these days.

Workbench – For weeding, taping and applying vinyl to substrates.

The size and type will be dependant on your own particular circumstances. Section 3 of this book describes in detail how to build your own custom work bench.

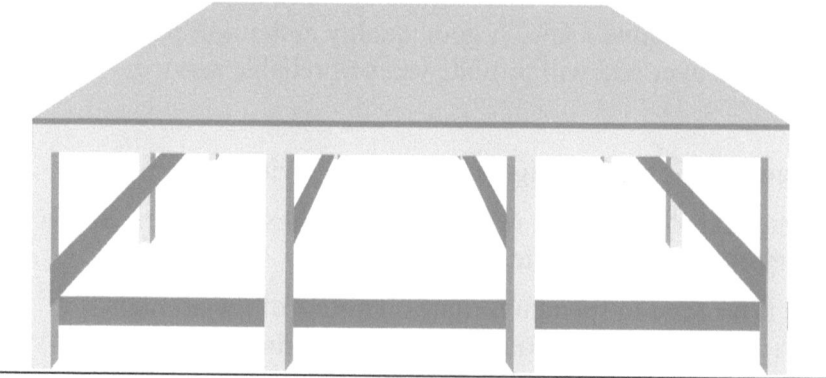

Sign Substrate Cutting Tools – For cutting boards – this could be a simple craft knife and steel rule, a table saw, or wall saw, or a dedicated sign substrate cutting device such as an Excalibur.

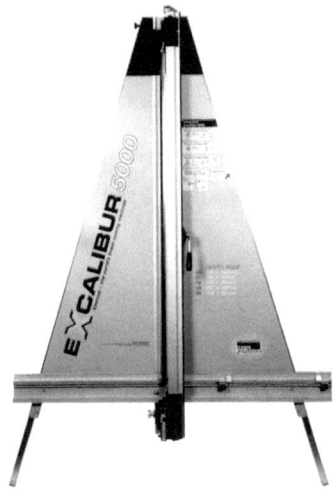

Applicator – For Applying vinyl. There are a number of different types available. Many vinyl manufacturers give simple rigid plastic applicators away with their vinyls or charge a nominal fee for these. Other more expensive applicators are available including soft felt applicators that avoid scratching un taped vinyls.

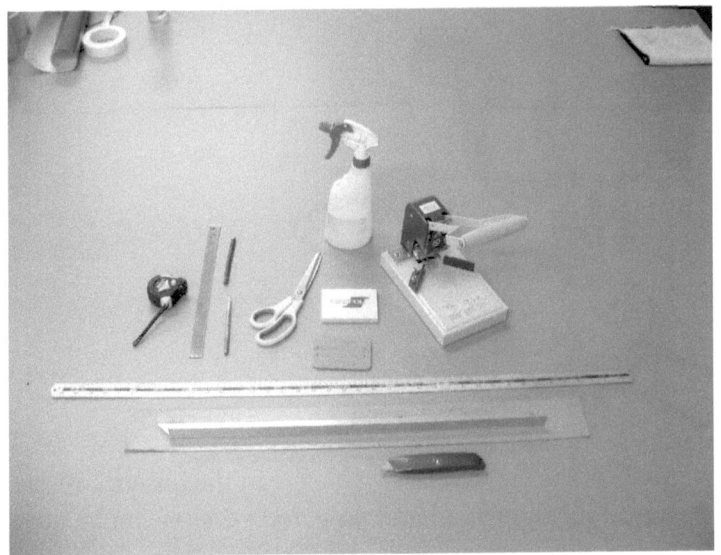

(Previous picture) typical handtools used every day. These include - tape measure, ruler, scalpel, crayon, scissors, squeegee, water spray, corner rounder, Straight edge (for cutting), craft knife.

Soft pencils or chinagraph crayons are used for marking up the substrates when laying up vinyl.

Cleaning tools – detergent, glue remover, rags, sponges, Chamois leather (for drying off vehicle paintwork)

Hot air gun (or even a hair dryer will do) used for heating vinyl into recesses and/or removing vinyl from substrates.

Desirable equipment (but not strictly necessary) for the new start sign business

Corner Rounder (see previous picture – top right)

Mitre Saw - for cutting sign trim (e.g. below powered version) Aluminium extrusions need to be cut to length and mitred to produce sign frames (see later chapter)

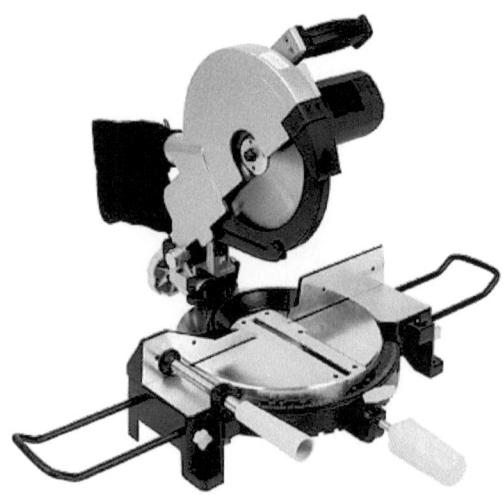

In the absence of an electric powered mitre saw, a hand powered version can be used instead.

Above - Hand powered mitre saw

Table saw (below) or wall saw

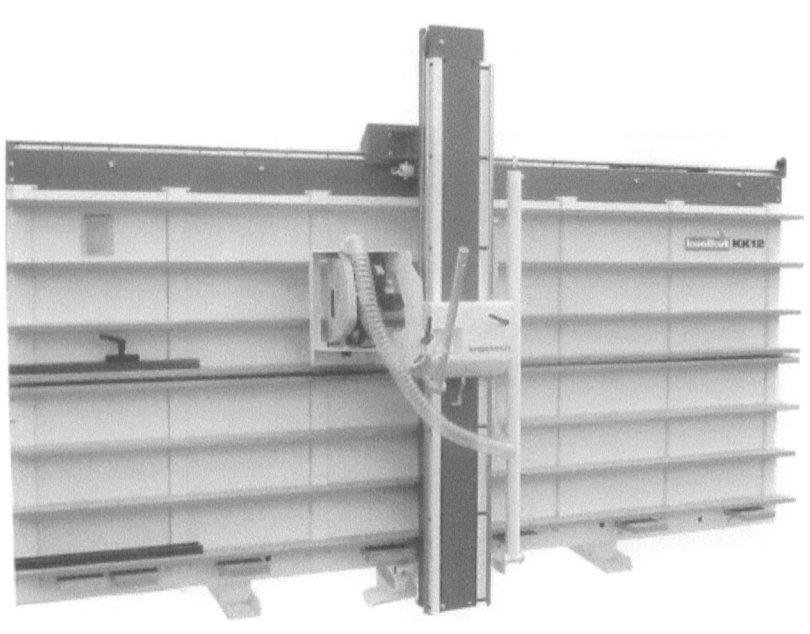

Above – Typical Wall Saw

The typical signmaker will have to cut a range of materials. Many of these can be cut by hand using a simple craft knife and straight edge. However, the job is made much easier if using a tailor made solution such as the Excalibur substrate cutting tool. This device will cut through a whole range of materials without producing any dust. Its major drawback is its limited cutting length. The largest of these machines will only cut a length of 1500mm (or so) which means the typical 8ft x 4ft sheet material cannot be cut lengthways. An alternative is to use a table saw which will cut any length of material. However, the drawback with these tools is they produce a lot of dust and can be hazardous for the untrained user.

The ultimate tool is surely the vertical panel saw which will cut just about every type of substrate a signmaker could wish for. The panel saw will cut length ways as well as vertically. They usually have a dust extraction system to keep dust particles in the atmosphere to a minimum. Their major drawback is their cost and the amount of space they need.

As well as equipment used for manufacturing, the typical signmaker will also require some essential office equipment to enable them to run the admin side to their business.

Office Equipment

PC – for writing letters and maintaining accounts. This need not be a high specification machine. Most entry level machines will do just about everything required to administer your business. Typically, providing internet access and email, along with accounts and word processing facilities. Business plans and pricing structures can also be drawn up with the aid of a suitable spreadsheet.

Telephones – Essential for any business (mobile and permanent land lines). When advertising your company always include your permanent land line number. Companies that exist with only a mobile number as a contact tend to inspire suspicion in the potential customers mind .

Fax Machine – ideally with it's own dedicated land line. Nowadays with the increasing use of email, fax machines are gradually becoming obsolete. However, for the moment at least, many businesses continue to use faxes to transmit and receive information.

Filing Cabinet – You will need a cabinet to keep all of your paper work in order. Nowadays this is perhaps not quite as essential as it used to be since most information will be stored on computer. However, suppliers catalogues, delivery notes and a whole range of other documents need to be stored in a way that they can be easily found and accessed.

Accounts software – Accounts software is becoming essential for any modern business. A decent package will help you to run your business much more efficiently. A modern package will allow you to build up a database of all your customers, as well as keeping track of all financial transactions.

Word processor – You will need this to write letters and produce any documents needed to run your company effectively.

Spreadsheet – for pricing work and for producing a cashflow forecast when writing your business plan.

Photocopier/Printer – a reasonably cheap combination printer/photocopier is all that you really need as discussed earlier.

Desk and Chair – Somewhere to sit and work when designing signs and performing administration duties.

Many of the tools and equipment mentioned in this chapter will already be present in the typical household. My advice for anyone starting a new business is to only buy equipment and furniture that is strictly necessary. It's very easy at the planning stages to get carried away and produce a list of essential tools and equipments when in reality you can start off with very little. When we first started we spent hundreds of pounds on a photocopying machine that we rarely used. This money would have been better utilised to aid our cashflow in the early days. Think twice before paying extravagant prices for furniture and equipment that is of secondary value and non essential to your business needs. Only later, once you have become successful, can you be justified in splashing out on that expensive furniture that you would like to have in your office.

Section 3 – Building a work bench

My workbench was designed for me by my late Father back in 1996 when I first set up my business. It measures 10ft x 6ft made from wood and mdf and is fitted with a grey 3mm plastic work top made from grey Forex.

The design is deliberately simple (it had to be for me to be able to construct it) yet is very robust and cheap to make. (I regularly stand on it without any problems). The bench is now more than twelve years old and has served me well. I expect it to go on serving me for many more years without any problems.

What follows is my updated version of the same design:-

This would measure 8ft x 6ft (2440mm x 1830mm) which is a reasonable size. The design can easily be adapted to produce a work bench (or series of work benches) of literally any size you choose.

The bench can be built using the simplest of hand tools. You will need a saw (for cutting to length and cutting the "steps on the legs described later). A simple hand saw will do but if you have access to a band saw or table saw this would speed up the process. The only other tools required are a drill, screwdriver, and countersink tool for countersinking the screw holes to allow the screw heads to remain flush with the surface . The sheet material (mdf and Forex) can often be bought ready cut to size

Materials Required (per bench – measuring 8ft x 6ft)

Planed Timber

2 lengths of 2440mm x 18mm x 94mm

2 lengths of 2404mm x 18mm x 94mm

6 lengths of 1830mm x 18mm x 94mm

2 lengths of 1798mm x 18mm x 94mm

10 lengths of 800mm x 70mm x 70mm

MDF

1 sheet 2440mm x 1220mm x18mm mdf

1 sheet 2440mm x 610mm x 18mm mdf

Worksurface

1 sheet 2440mm x 1220mm x 3mm Grey pvc (e.g. Forex)

1 sheet 2440mm x 610mm x 3mm Grey pvc (e.g. Forex)

(The reason for specifying grey Forex is that the coloured Forex is tougher and more durable than ordinary white board – it also looks better and is less likely to show up marks than white board)

Step 1

The first job is to cut the 10 legs that will support the bench.. These are made from good quality planed timber each measuring 800mm x 70mm x 70mm. This size provides a very strong support and will result in a bench height that is ideal for someone of average height. (the resultant height off the ground of the completed bench will be 821mm).

Each leg must have "steps" cut into the top as shown in the diagram. (These "steps" are to support the perimeter rails). You will need six legs of one type (regular legs) and four of the other type (these fit at the four corners of the bench).

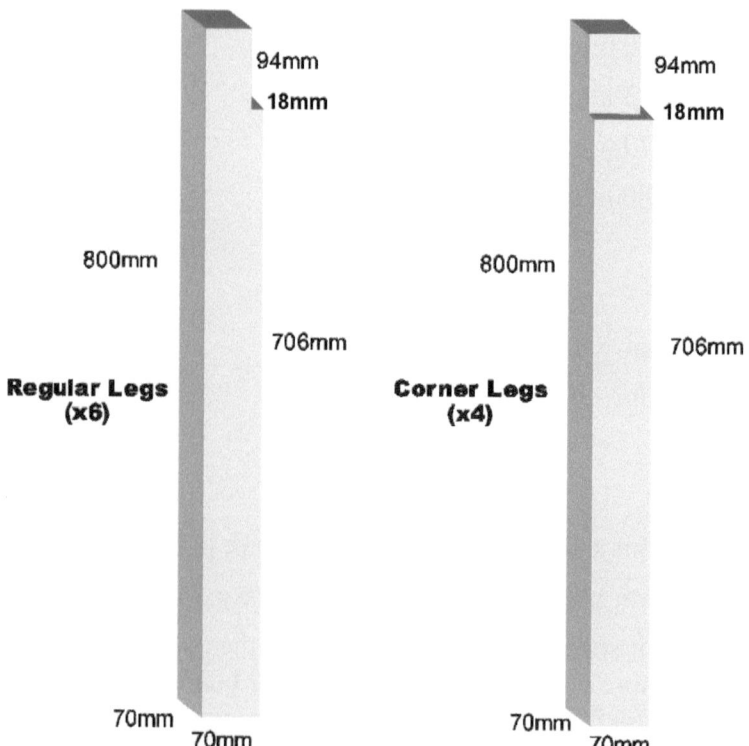

(Diagram showing the six regular and four corner legs that will support the work bench)

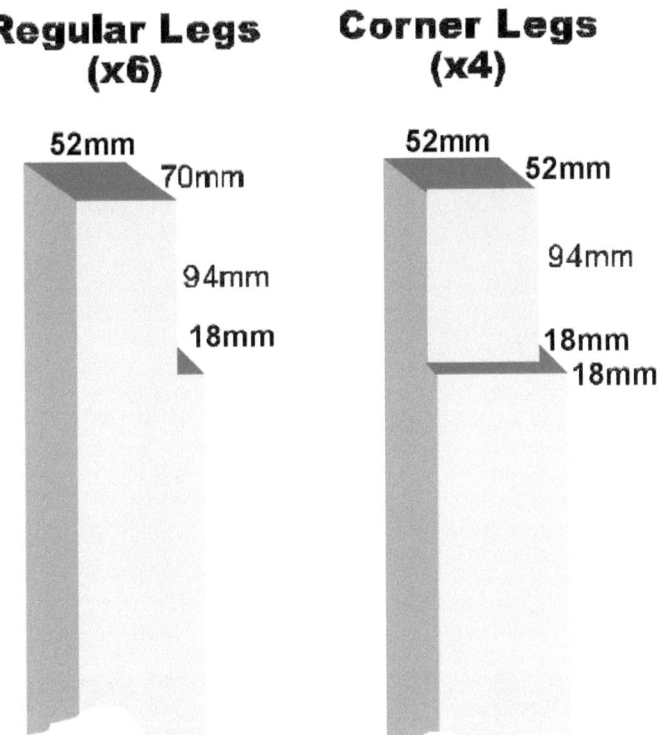

Top of leg details

(Close up showing the "steps" that must be cut into the top of each leg)

Step 2

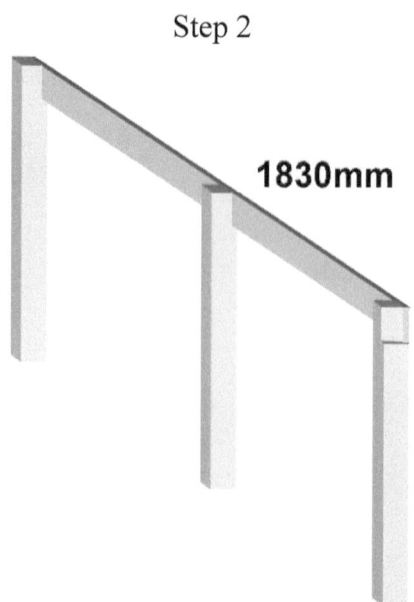

1830mm

Take two corner legs, and one regular leg and attach these to a perimeter rail as shown. The perimeter rail is made from a length of planed timber measuring 1830mm x 94mm x 18mm. Each leg is screwed to the perimeter rails using two woodscrews (one at the top left, and one at the bottom right of each "step"). Drill a pilot hole for each screw before inserting to prevent the wood from splitting. Also remember to counter sink each hole so that the top of the screw is level with the wood surface once it has been fitted

Step 3

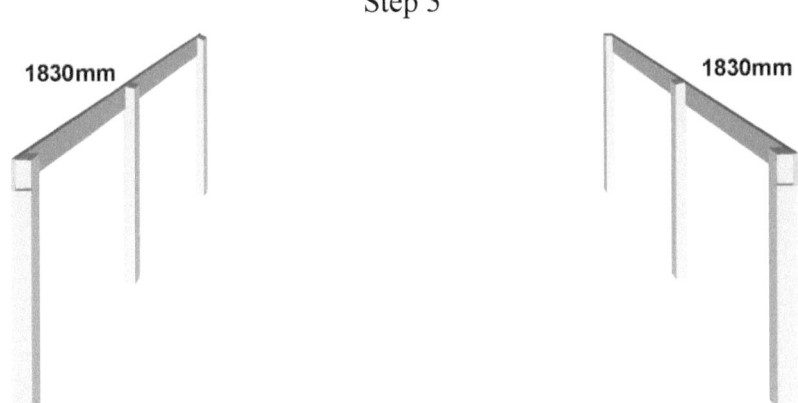

Repeat step 2 to produce the opposite end to the work bench as shown above.

Step 4

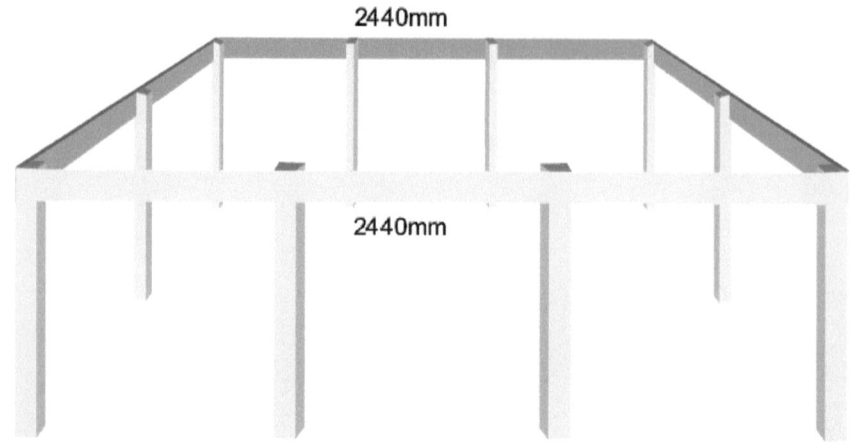

Now join the two opposite ends of the work bench by linking these together with two more perimeter rails this time measuring 2404mm x 94mm x 18mm (giving a total length of 2440mm when you include the thickness of the two end rails). Then attach a further four (two on each side) regular legs one third and two thirds along the length of the perimeter rail as shown in the diagram above and picture below.

Step 5

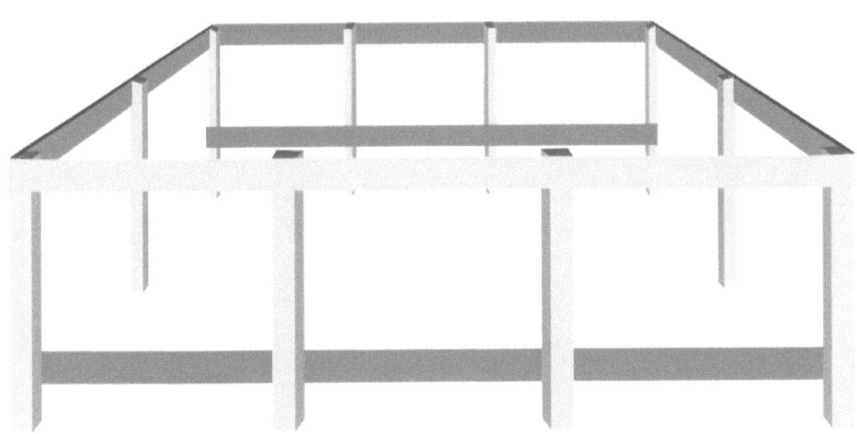

Now attach lower rails running the length of the bench as shown. These measure 2440mm x 94mm x 18mm . They are screwed onto the inside of each leg approximately 4 to 6 inches up from ground level.

Step 6

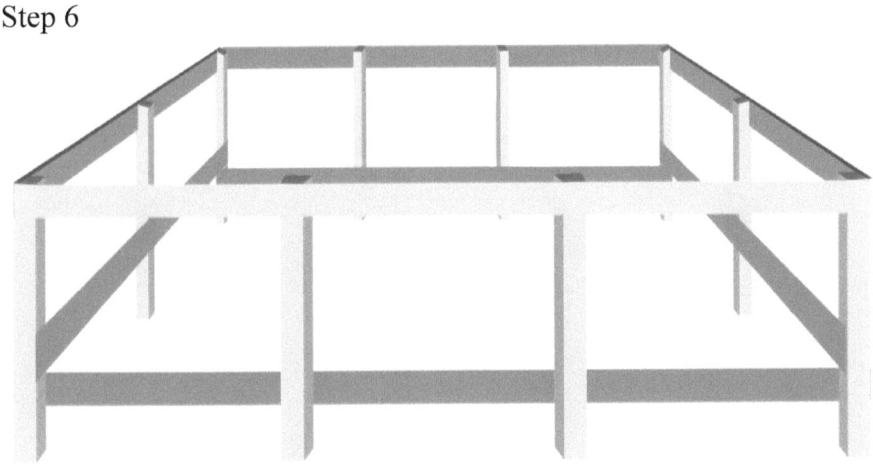

Next attach lower rails measuring 1830mm x 94mm x 18mm running the width of the bench. These rails sit above the lower rails previously fitted as shown in the diagram above

Step 7

To provide internal support to the work surface, attach two top rails measuring 1794mm x 94mm x 18mm between the two inner legs as shown in the picture above. Also attach two lower rails measuring 1830mm x 94mm x 18mm between the two inner legs as shown in the diagram beow

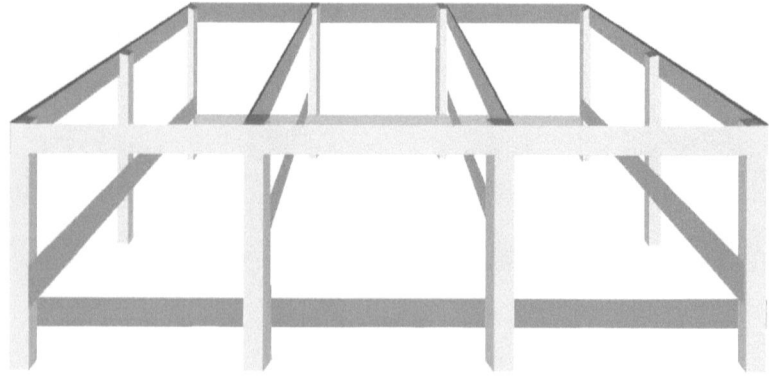

Step 8

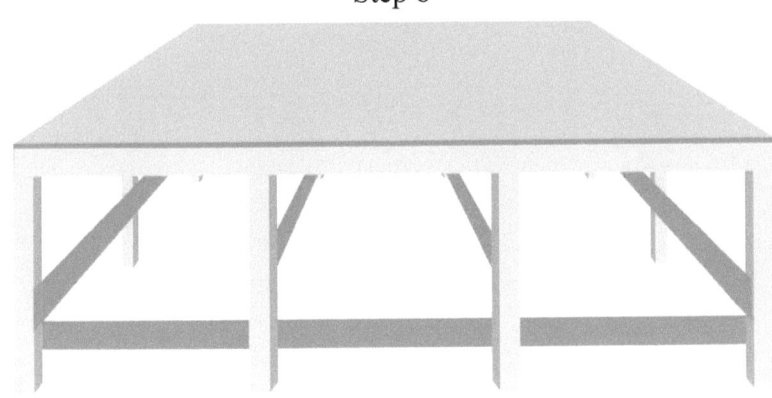

The bench is completed by placing the 18mm MDF on top of the workbenches frame. The flat MDF panels are held in place by woodscrews fastened along the perimeter of the bench. If desired you can fit shelves on the lower rails as shown on the picture below. These shelves consist of 12mm MDF measuring 2440mm x 610mm.

At this stage the bench can be varnished (allow at least two coats – rubbing down between each coat). Then finally attach the top PVC grey top work surface (again using woodscrews along the perimeter of the bench).

Section 4 – Sign Software

Vector Drawing Packages – Computer cut vinyl

The main method used in signmaking is a system known as computer cut vinyl . Vinyl cut lettering and logos are designed on a computer using one of a variety of software packages that are available. Sign design software uses "vector drawing" imagery for producing layouts. "Vector drawn" images are a series of shapes (described mathematically in the computers memory) making up the design (as opposed to thousands of different coloured individual pixels which are used to represent rendered images such as photographs). If you wish to design signs forget about using graphics packages such as MS paint or even Photoshop. These packages do not produce vector drawn graphics

Wireframe version of a vector drawn image of a pentagon

This is the painted (or coloured in) version of the shape shown above

This example is of a low resolution **rendered** image. In this case you can see the edges of the shape appear ragged, whereas in the "mathematically described" vector drawn version of the same image the edges are completely smooth.

These types of images can be infinitely scaled up with no deterioration in quality since they are not subject to the limits of resolution that a rendered image has. Rendered images can not be cut from vinyl and can only ever be represented by printing them, whereas vector images can be both cut and printed. MS paint and Photoshop produce rendered graphics – so forget about these types of design packages for now.

Above - an even lower resolution version of the same image. This serves to illustrate even further the limitations of resolution in "rendered" images.

These vector drawn shapes (e.g. individual letters making up each word) are then produced in self adhesive vinyl by sending the cutting information to a plotter driven by the computer which traces the letters (or shapes) onto the vinyl surface using a cutting knife. These letters are then transferred to any suitable surface using an application tape (sometimes known as transfer paper). The key element in the entire process is the vinyl cutter which is driven by the computer.

Even complex designs can be achieved using a combination of vinyl colours The computer cut vinyl method of making signs is much quicker and cost effective than the traditional signwriting (painting) method.

Examples of Vector drawing software.

One of the most well known packages used by Signmakers is Signlab. This software was designed specifically for the Sign designer and Signmaker. It has all the necessary tools to allow you to create signs in vinyl. Amongst the many features that are highly desirable is the ability to apply a range of shadows and distortions to lettering. "Signlab" features allow the images to be combined into a simple shape discarding all of the unnecessary paths that may have made up the original image but which are not required at the cutting stage (indeed additional vector paths sometimes present in the wireframe version of the image being worked on are undesirable at the cutting stage). Signlab also contains vectorising tools which allow rendered images such as bmp, tiff and jpg files to be converted from images consisting of thousands of tiny pixels making up the image into a series of straight lines and curves making up the image that can consequently be trace cut into vinyl sheets. Finally, Signlab software integrates seamlessly with a whole range of plotter and router equipment allowing the signmaker to use the software to design his work then send it directly to the vinyl cutter.

There are also many other software packages that contain the types of features that are dedicated to signmakers. These included Flexisign and Vinyl Master Pro. These software packages are piracy protected by the use of software keys or Dongles. Typically, a dongle is a hardware key that plugs into a serial or USB port. The software package is designed to recognise whether or not this key is present on the computer trying to run the application. Should the software key not be found, the sign program simply shuts down. Consequently, this type of software can only be run on one computer at any one time. An additional software license must be purchased if the application is to be run simultaneously on different computers. In some cases a design only version of the program can be purchased (at lower cost) to allow a second design station to be operated independent of the computer that would also control the vinyl cutter. Dedicated sign software is very powerful and contains many useful features that allow the signmaker to work productively. This type of application is relatively expensive but will pay for itself many times over due to the productivity gains it gives the signmaker over lesser non dedicated sign software.

There are of course other vector drawing packages that are not industry specific (i.e. not dedicated sign making software). Amongst these are Corel Draw and Adobe Illustrator. These applications are designed for desk top publication but are equally at home in sign design due to the fact they produce vector drawn graphics. Some may argue that they do not contain the many tools and shortcuts present in sign specific software but they are advancing all the time and often contain their own unique features that may not be present in dedicated sign making applications. Whilst dedicated sign software such as Signlab has clear advantages, anyone working on a tight budget may wish to consider using a cheaper application such as Corel draw to design their signs.

In recent years a new system for making signs has entered the market. This is the combined digital printer /contour cutting device. These recent machines look set to make great inroads into the main method of sign making. With their combination of digital printing and contour cutting, they are capable of producing signs much quicker and more highly detailed than cut vinyl alone could ever do. Further more, they can print rendered images (such as photographs) that can't be realised using vinyl cutting methods.

But for the moment, computer cut vinyl still remains the predominant method of producing signs and this looks likely to remain so for the foreseeable future.

Rendered image and photo manipulation software – Digital Printing

If you are already a master of Photoshop and consequently have decided to become a signmaker to utilise these skills, don't despair at what you have read so far! Photoshop skills will stand you in good stead much later when your business evolves into digital print.

But first and foremost you must master a vector drawing package if you wish to become a signmaker.

Section 5 – Substrates

What is a "substrate"? Quite simply the substrate is the backing material making up the sign. For a plastic or metal sign it is the plastic or metal backing. Or in the case of a van livery, it is the van itself.

There are many different substrates used in signmaking. Here is a short guide to some of them:-

Plastics

A number of different plastics are used as sign substrates. Some of the most commonly used are as follows:-

Foam PVC (Typical brand names for this type of plastic include Forex, and Foamalux).

This is a lightweight foam PVC material. It is relatively inexpensive and looks attractive making it an ideal substrate. These boards come in a range of standard sizes and thicknesses. Ranging from 1mm, 2mm, 3mm, 5mm, and 10mm thicknesses. Board sizes are typically 2440 x 1220mm, or 3050mm x 1500mm. This material is commonly used for a whole range of sign types including interior and exterior use. When used outdoors it generally requires to be fitted using signtrim (see later in this book) to allow the material to expand and contract without warping when subject to temperature changes. These boards are available with either a matt or gloss finish. They are also available in a range of colours. However, coloured boards with a matt finish are not well suited to outdoor use for anything other than short term as the colours will quickly fade. The gloss versions are much more colour fast and so are suited to outdoor use long term (white boards are not affected by colour fade). This material is fairly fragile and can be easily damaged. It can be easily cut by hand using a simple craft knife (though the gloss versions have a much tougher finish making them more difficult to cut by hand).

Corrugated (or fluted) plastic (common brand name Corex).

This is a corrugated plastic similar in appearance to corrugated cardboard. Most commonly used for estate agents signs. This material is very inexpensive yet is tough and durable making it ideal for outdoor use. Due to its corrugations it is less attractive than smooth plastic substrates such as foam PVC for example, but is ideal for cheap high volume signs required at low cost. Available in a range of thicknesses and board sizes. Corrugated plastic is easily cut using a craft knife.

Acrylic – (Common brand names include perspex).

Acrylic is much more expensive material than foam PVC or fluted plastics. It has a high gloss appearance and is very tough and durable. However, as with Foam PVC, it is liable to expand and contract when heated so needs to be fitted using signtrim when used outdoors. These boards have a high gloss finish and are available in a range of colours which are colour fast and not prone to fading when fitted outdoors. The material is very hard but also quite brittle. It cannot be cut by hand very easily and usually needs a mechanical saw to cut the sheet. Acrylic is used much less commonly nowadays with the advent of gloss foam PVC materials which are much cheaper yet very similar in appearance. However, clear acrylic and opal acrylic are used for illuminated signs.

Metals

Aluminium – this is an ideal choice for traffic signs and high quality signs of all types. Special cutting equipment is required for fabrication. Aluminium can be powder coated. This metal does not warp when used outdoors.

Aluminium/polyethylene composite material (common brand names include Dibond, Alucolor, Skybond).

These products consist of a polyethylene core sandwiched between thin aluminium faces. This is a fairly recent development and is often used in place of traditional aluminium signs. Available in a range of thicknesses and sizes. (typical sheet size 2440mm x 1220mm x 3mm). Also available in a range of colours and in Matt or Gloss finish. The material is relatively easy to cut – and can even be cut (though with some difficulty) using a craft knife.

This product can also be routed and folded to produce signtrays.

Flexible Substrates

Banner – Nylon reinforced PVC

This is a flexible "tarpaulin" like material used to produce banners. It can be printed on or lettered using computer cut vinyl (special banner vinyls are available that are designed to flex with the substrate).

Magnetic Sheeting

Magnetic sheeting is used mainly for vehicle signs. The magnetic sheeting comes in rolls (usually 610mm wide) with a white vinyl face ready for vinyl graphics. Magnetic sheeting is easily cut using a craft knife and straight edge (ruler). It can even be cut using scissors.

Whenever I sell a set of magnetic signs I always print off the following letter of advice. This gives the client important information in the use and care of magnetic signs. I would strongly recommend you do something similar both to inform your customer, and to minimise any comeback to you (as the vendor) if the user should experience any problems with the use of their magnetic signs. The inclusion of this advice also demonstrates to you client that you care and enhances your "professionalism" in the eye of the customer

.

TIPS FOR USING MAGNETIC SIGNS

ATTACHING

The attaching surfaces of both the vehicle and the magnetic plates must be dry and free of dust.

Hold the magnetic plate above the appropriate surface and let go; do not slide (to prevent scratches)

Do not apply over decorative mouldings or sharp contoured folds.

Never apply the magnetic sign to a newly sprayed, painted or polished surface; let the paintwork harden properly first.

CARE

Clean with a mild detergent only; never use aggressive agents.

And do not forget the attaching surfaces; a layer of dirt considerably reduces the magnetic adhesive power.

STORAGE

The magnetic sign must be stored flat to prevent "donkey's ears" eg against a flat metal cabinet or wall (never against a heater or a contoured surface)

Do not leave it loose in the vehicle; the material may become deformed.

Do not roll up more tightly than diameter 10cm, always with the magnetic side facing inwards.

GENERAL

In summer temperatures and where there is continuous use of the signs on the vehicle over many days, under certain conditions they may become stuck to the paintwork. To avoid this risk, the magnetic plates should be removed when not being used or at night. During the day take off the magnetic signs at least once and re-attach them.

Attaching surfaces of vehicles which have obviously been filled or sprayed several times considerably reduce the magnetic adhesive power.

The plastic film is sensitive to pressure; handle with great care.

Cracks and tears can occur only as a result of careless handling.

Section 6 – Vinyls & Cutting Basics

A computer cut vinyl sign making system would comprise of the following key elements.

1/ Computer

2/ Software – Vector drawing package (e.g. Signlab, Corel Draw, Adobe Illustrator etc.) Prices range from £200 to about £3,000 depending on the software chosen.

3/ Vinyl Cutter – this could be a standalone vinyl cutter such as a Summagraphics or Roland device, or could be part of a combination digital printing/vinyl cutting system such as the Roland Versacamm. Prices range from £500 (for a second hand or non branded Chinese made cutter) to about £3,000 for a quality vinyl cutter, or £8,000 for a combined digital printer/cutting device

4/ Artwork Libraries – There are a number of artwork libraries available for the sign maker. One of the most useful is the vehicle outline library. These are discs containing vector drawn files of commercial vehicles that allow the sign maker to produce vehicle livery designs on full size templates without ever actually seeing the customers vehicle. Other useful libraries include safety signs (standard safety sign designs).

Prices for a comprehensive vehicle outline package start at about £100 and you can often get very good deals from the companies that produce these libraries by buying a number of libraries (vehicle outlines, safety signs etc.) in one comprehensive package.

5/ Scanner – This is used to scan existing designs to "get them into the computer memory" so that the images can be vectorised (converted into a format that can be cut) and manipulated using the sign design software. There is no need to spend much money on a scanner. Scanners costing as little as £50 are more than adequate for the purpose

6/ Desktop Inkjet Printer – these are not used to produce the actual signs, but are used to allow the designer to print out the proposed layout to allow his (or her) clients to approve the sign designs. With the advent of email this is becoming less and less of a basic requirement as designs are now often emailed directly to the client for approval. A basic colour printer can be bought for as little as £30 these days.

Nowadays there are good quality inkjet printers that also combine photocopying and scanning features.

Nowadays it is possible to put together a basic sign making system for under £1000. But for someone planning a more serious venture I would suggest budgeting in the region of £5,000 for a reasonable quality vinyl cutting setup – and about £10,000 for a combination system that included digital printing and computer cut vinyl.

Vinyl Types

Calendered Vinyl

There are basically two types of Calendered vinyls available. These are Monomeric and Polymeric films.

Monomeric vinyls are low cost material made using a lower molecular weight plasticiser making this type of film best suited to short term outdoor applications as well as indoor use. This type of vinyl is quite prone to shrinkage.

Polymeric calendered vinyls are made using a higher molecular weight plasticiser which means the film is well suited to outdoor use (these are less likely to shrink than monomeric vinyl). More recently high performance polymeric calendered vinyls have been introduced which have similar properties to the generally more expensive cast versions discussed later. These high performance films are much thinner and perform well when applied to difficult surfaces such as those containing rivets.

Generally speaking high performance polymeric calendered vinyls are a good all round product for general use.

They are made by rolling a "dough like" mixture of PVC with various plasticisers, pigments resins and lubricants through a series of heated rollers which gradually produces a finer and finer film until it reaches it's final thickness. The film is then given either a gloss or matt finish by passing it through either a highly polished or matt finish roller. This part of the process is called embossing. Finally the finished product is allowed to cool down again by passing over and under a series of cooling rollers.

Because the vinyl has been produced by rolling it out, it has a natural tendency to try and revert back to its original shape (this is what causes it to shrink). On the plus side, because of the way the material has been produced (i.e. by rolling) it has a higher tensile strength than cast vinyl and as a result is less prone to tearing making it easier to remove.

Cast Vinyl

Cast vinyl (as the name suggests) is made from a liquid mixture of PVC resins, solvents, pigments plasticizers and additives. This mixture (called an Organosol) is poured or coated onto a casting paper. This is then slowly passed through a very long oven which causes the solvents to evaporate from the Organosol leaving a solid dry film on top of the casting paper. It has a lower tensile strength then calendered and consequently is much more conformable and capable of stretching. These properties make the material ideal for vehicle graphics where a high performance is required such as stretching and fitting into deep recesses or fitting over rivets.

However, the production process is much slower which makes cast films more expensive than their calendered cousins.

As a general rule, it's fair to say you get what you pay for. The cheaper the product, the poorer it's performance and longevity. However, there are instances where the properties of a high performance calendered vinyls are better suited to certain applications then even cast films.

As a good all rounder – I prefer to use a high performance polymeric calendered product.

Transluscent Vinyl

Transluscent vinyl is (as the name suggest) a film that allows light to pass through. Consequently it is used for illuminated backlit signs. These films can be either Cast or Calendered . However, due to the heating and cooling they experience in their lifetime they do need to be a high performance material.

Reflective Vinyl

Reflective vinyl reflects light and so glows at night when a light shines upon it. Typically they are used in road signs (where the cars headlights cause the sign to light up) and for emergency vehicle markings.

There are two types of reflective material.:-

Class 1 reflective is used on road signs as well as police cars and ambulances. This material has a highly visible honeycomb appearance and is very difficult to cut. Indeed it is not designed to be used with a conventional plotter (a normal sign cutter is simply not capable of cutting Class 1 reflective) and requires a flatbed cutter to enable it to be cut into shapes.

Class 2 reflective is less highly reflective than Class 1 but is much more user friendly for the typical sign shop. An ordinary cutter will cut this material though the lifespan of the cutting knife will be dramatically reduced. In appearance it is very similar to ordinary vinyl and is available in a range of colours. Reflective vinyls are more expensive than normal films and can be more difficult to weed and remove again later on.

There are a number of rules and regulations that apply to the use of these markings on vehicles. Consequently it is prudent to advise clients to check that any intended used of reflective signs on their vehicles do not breach any legislation.

Fluorescent Vinyl

Fluorescent vinyls literally glow in the dark. They do this not by reflecting light in the same way as reflective vinyls but by absorbing light and then emitting it again at a different wavelength. Thus white light or even ultraviolet light can be used to make a fluorescent vinyl glow. Fluorescent films are easily spotted having very distinctive glowing colours such as pink, orange and bright yellow/green.

These vinyls have a very limited lifetime due to the fact that the fluorescent nature of the film is caused by a chemical reaction. This chemistry quickly reduces in time giving lifetimes of only a few months in exterior use. Eventually the fluorescent property of the material disappears altogether which makes these films only suitable for short term use.

Phosphorescent Vinyl

Phosphorescent vinyls are mainly used in the production of fire safety signs. This material literally does "glow in the dark" (unlike Fluorescent material which only glows when there is a visible or UV light source shining on it). It works by absorbing visible or UV light which causes the electrons surrounding the molecules of the pigment to become excited. As a result these electrons jump to a higher orbit thus containing more energy. When the light source is removed, the electrons gradually return to their former state (lower energy orbit) and in the process of doing so they give off visible light causing the material to glow for an extended period until all of the electrons have returned to their former (pre-excited) state.

Phosphorescent vinyl is effectively "charged up" during daylight hours, and gradually discharges (gives off light) when the daylight is removed. This is not an electrical or radioactive process but is merely a physical property of the pigment used. Consequently there are no safety issues attributed to the use of these materials.

Unlike Fluorescent films, Phosphorescent vinyl has an extended lifetime and will continue to work for many years.

Etch Vinyl

Etch vinyls are used to produce an etched (or frosted) effect when applied to glass. They are transluscent (usually silvery grey – but also available in silvery pink, gold and blue hues). Once applied they give glass the appearance of being expensively etched.

Metallic and Prismatic Vinyl

These types can be used to create many eyecatching effects. Chrome finish metallic versions are readily available and relatively cheap. In addition there are prismatic vinyls that are actually embossed to give a textured look. Finally there are micro embossed metallic vinyls that have fine grid patterns that cause diffraction patterns when viewed in natural light. These fine grid lines create rainbow effects and 3d patterns that can look stunning.

Banner Vinyl

Banner vinyl is specifically designed for applying to nylon reinforced banners. This type of vinyl is much softer and more flexible and is designed to prevent tunneling when applied to a banner. Ordinary films can be used but only if the banner is to be used short term.

Medium and long term banners should always be decorated using proper banner vinyls.

Print Vinyl

In most cases, general purpose print vinyls are based around their normal vinyl counterparts. The only difference being they are produced with a scrupulously clean surface.

Clear Vinyl – Laminates

Clear vinyls are mainly used to provide a clear laminate protection over print. They can also be used to produce printed stickers to fit on the inside of a glass panel to be viewed from outside. However, printing on clear using ordinary inks (CMYK) produces a very weak image due to the absence of the white background. Therefore, it is usual to laminate a clear printed sticker with a white vinyl to create a white background which allows the image to be seen correctly and stand out.

Other uses for clear vinyl are to provide abrasion resistance to various substrates (e.g a cars painted bodywork).

Rapid air /Easy Apply

With the increasing popularity of vinyl wrapping, manufacturers have turned their attentions to finding ways to make the application process easier. This has resulted in the development of easy apply and rapid air vinyl that have a glue coating specifically designed to make the elimination of bubbles during application much easier. These vinyls have an embossed pattern in the glue. This embossing allows a series of channels to exist in the glue coating that allows the air to escape when the applicator is pulled across the surface. The resultant effect is similar to applying ordinary vinyl to a painted wood grain surface. (The grain in the wood provides a series of small groves that allow the air to escape in much the same way as the tiny grooves in the glue surface allows the air to escape).

Weeding and Taping

Weeding is the term used to describe the removal of the excess vinyl after cutting. Once the cutter has performed its part in the process the sheet is removed from the cutter and placed on a workbench ready for the next stage in the process. Using a scalpel or pair of tweezers, the operator now is required to remove all of the excess material left over after the shapes of the lettering and/or graphics have been trace cut into the vinyl by the plotter.

Most right handed people prefer to work from right to left when removing vinyl. whereas left handed individuals tend to prefer working from left to right. Letters such as "E,F,G,L,C and K" are best weeded from left to right to minimise parts of the letters from lifting away from the backing paper. Therefore many right handed people if working from right to left may find it easier to turn the lettering upside down when weeding.

Here you can see the excess vinyl being pulled away from the backing sheet leaving the cut shapes (letters) in place

Once the excess vinyl has been pulled from the backing paper the remaining pieces of vinyl (the inner parts of the "O,B Q" etc.) also need to be removed. This is best done with the point of a scalpel blade.

With practice, a skilled operator can carry out weeding at a very fast rate. Much faster than seems possible the first time the process is attempted by the novice signmaker.

With the excess removed the next step in the process is to apply the application tape. The application tape is used to lift all of the individual lettering off the backing paper to allow it to be transferred to the surface of the substrate. There are a number of different types of application tapes available. These come in a range of tacs (low medium, high) as well as clear or opaque. The tape is first unrolled and then placed on top of of the weeded vinyl

The tape is then stuck firmly to the lettering by applying pressure with a squeegee over the application tape and scraping the paper down onto the surface

The final step is to remove the tape from the application paper leaving the lettering in place and the sticky side of the vinyl exposed. This is best done by turning the sheet face down onto the workbench (so that the application tape is in contact with the top of the bench) then carefully peeling away the backing paper leaving the lettering attached to the tape. Done this way there is less likelihood of letters remaining on the backing paper rather than being transferred to the tape

With the lettering and glue side exposed the next step is to apply the cut vinyl to the substrate which is described next.

Section 7 - Vinyl application techniques

There are two main methods for applying vinyl. These are wet application and dry application. Each method has its own advantages and disadvantages. These are summarised as follows:-

Wet Application:-

Advantages

1/ Easy way to apply vinyl with good results. Ideal for the beginner.

2/ Once applied – the vinyl can still be removed and re-positioned (assuming the application tape has not yet been removed).

3/ Easy to apply in difficult conditions. e,g in windy conditions wet vinyl does not stick to itself when the wind catches it causing the sticky side to stick to itself.

4/ The "sticky" side of wet vinyl can be easily cleaned. Even vinyl that has been dropped can have grit removed from the sticky side by washing.

5/ Avoidance of "bubbles" of trapped air.

6/ Large sections can be laid roughly into position then slid into final postion before using the applicator.

Disadvantages

1/ Longer time required to wet and apply the graphics.

2/ The vinyl needs to dry out before the application tape can be removed.

3/ Difficult to apply into recesses since the wetted glue will not stick straight away.

Dry Application

Advantages

1/ Speedy application

2/ Can be stretched and applied over recesses and difficult surfaces.

3/ No waiting for the vinyl to dry before removing application tape

4/ Instant bonding with the substrate

Disadvantages

1/ Requires skill and practice to avoid bubbles

2/ Once the sticky side of vinyl clings to itself it is usually beyond rescuing

3/ Greater accuracy required when applying large sections. Once in position the graphic cannot be minutely adjusted by sliding it into a new position.

Generally speaking, for the experienced signmaker, dry application is the preferred method due to its simplicity and quickness. A van can be quickly applied dry in a fraction of the time it may take to do the work wet (with the consequent financial benefits of doing the job much quicker).

Wet Application – Method

Commercial application fluids can be purchased from suppliers of sign materials. These are specially formulated to dry very quickly and speed up the wet application method.

However, a perfectly suitable application fluid can be made up by mixing a few drops of washing up liquid with water. The detergent serves to break down the surface tension in the water. Without detergent the water will pool into droplets leaving much of the surface still dry. Use as little detergent as possible otherwise the time taken for the vinyl to dry will be lengthened.

First though, you need to mark the position where the vinyl lettering is to be placed.

In this example ,we are applying lettering to a vehicle. First we place a series of marks on the bodywork showing where the design should be placed. This is done using a crayon or soft pencil. Marks are placed on the bodywork after carefully measuring the position with a tape measure. The centre point is also marked.

Apply the application fluid to the sticky side of the vinyl. This is best done by spraying the fluid using a small plant water bottle sprayer.

Alternatively a sponge can be dipped into the fluid and wiped across the surface of the glue.

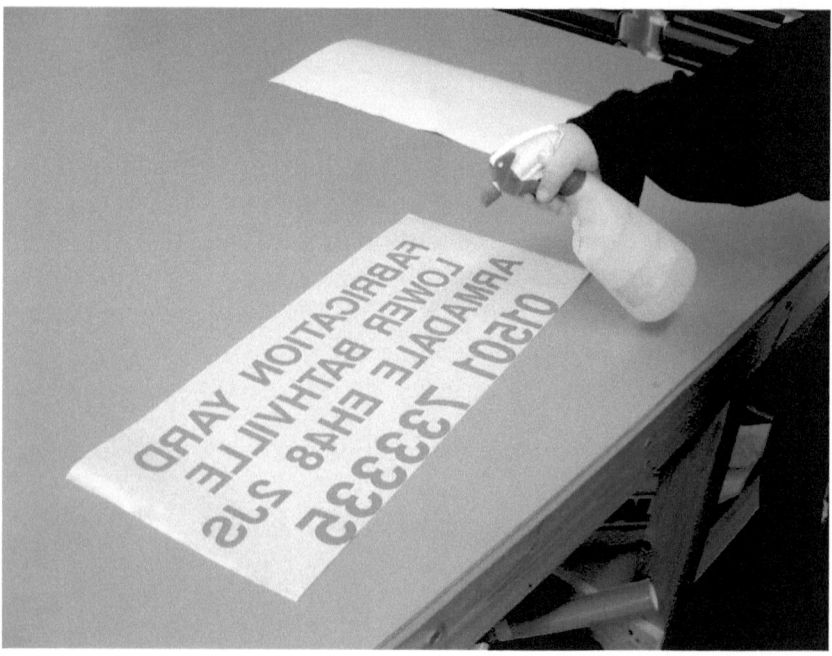

Next apply the application fluid onto the substrate.

Now offer the design into position on the substrate and smooth out the vinyl and application tape.

The top of the tape is aligned with the marks placed previously on the bodywork. Note also that the centre of the lettering being applied has been marked on the top of the tape. This is lined up with the centre point that had already been marked on the panel.

Using an applicator carefully squeegee over the entire surface of the tape. Try and work methodically to ensure no area is missed which will leave bubbles of water behind the vinyl.

Once all of the water has been squeegeed out, allow the graphics to dry for some time before trying to remove the tape. The length of time required will depend on the ambient temperature, the substrate being applied to, and the amount of detergent in the application fluid.

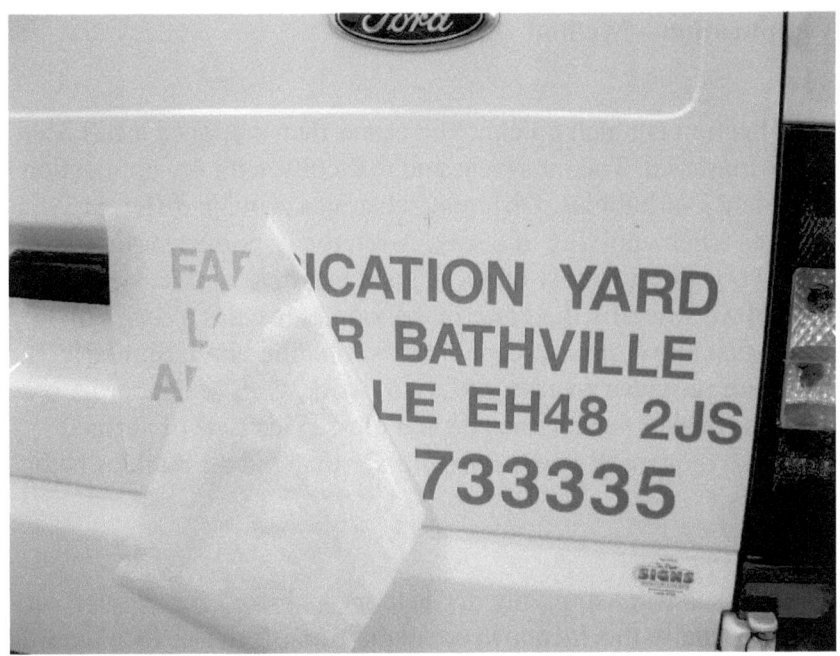

When first attempting to remove the tape check that the lettering is not lifting from the substrate. If it does lay it back down again, apply the applicator and wait a bit longer before trying again.

Typically when applying vinyl to a van you will need to wait fifteen minutes or so before attempting to remove the tape. At the other extreme (e.g. if applying vinyl wet to a window), you may have to leave the material twenty four hours before the tape can be removed without causing the lettering to lift.

If you time it right it is often possible to squeegee out any remaining bubbles of water trapped behind the vinyl discovered once the application tape has been removed. If the vinyl is too dry at this stage the water can be expelled by using a sharp blade to puncture the surface and allow the water to be expelled. Any small bubbles of trapped liquid will eventually disappear in a few days or so.

Dry application – Method

Dry application is much quicker and easier than wet once it has been properly mastered. The main fear and difficulty with dry application is the avoidance of bubbles. Different substrates provide different challenges when applying this way. A relatively porous surface is actually very easy to apply on to. A good example of this is a painted wood surface whereby the grain in the wood provides a series of channels that allow air to escape from behind the vinyl. Similarly, matt Foam board provides an easy surface to work with. Much harder are high gloss finishes such as acrylic and glass. This type of surface needs much more skill when applying dry to avoid air bubbles being trapped.

The main issue when applying dry is to try and work the vinyl in one direction. Usually this means keeping the film off the surface until the moment the squeegee blade passes over the vinyl causing it to make contact with the substrate.

When applying this way I often begin by removing the backing paper then placing it back down onto the glue surface while allowing an inch or so of application tape/exposed vinyl to remain unprotected by the backing paper.

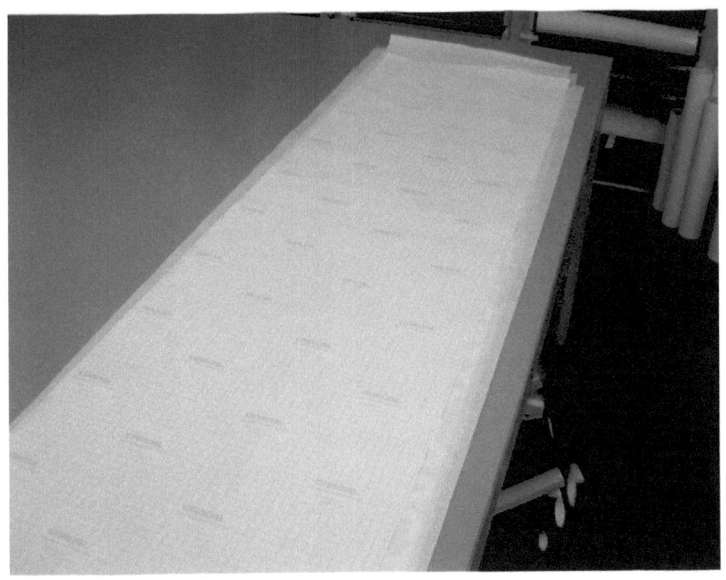

This small margin is then used to place the vinyl onto the substrate and allow it to stay in place.

Here you can see the pre-spaced lettering placed on the side of a vehicle held in place by the exposed top of the application tape. The lettering itself is prevented from sticking to the bodywork by the backing paper.

Larger pieces can be applied in sections simply by using a scissors to cut the design into smaller more manageable sections and removing one section of backing paper at a time allowing the other sections glue surfaces to remain protected by the backing paper that remains temporarily in place.

Here you can see one portion of the pre-spaced group being separated from the backing paper by hinging the application tape upwards and carefully removing.

Followed by holding the paper taut (and a fraction away from the bodywork) while going over the top with an applicator – to expel the air and apply pressure to the vinyl causing it to stick to the cars panel.

Where the lettering bridges part of the bodywork (e.g over a door shut) a scalpel is used to carefully cut through the bridged lettering **whilst ensuring the blade does not cut into the paintwork.**

Next the section of vinyl that bridges the gap is folded down onto the door shut return using the edge of the applicator.

Then the application tape is removed leaving the pre-spaced lettering in place.

The finished job – all done dry, but made easier by breaking it down into smaller sections as just described.

As with wet application – don't beat yourself up too much if you are left with a lot of trapped air bubbles. The worst of these can be removed by puncturing the vinyl and expelling the blister of air. If left for some time any small trapped air bubbles will eventually disappear after a few days.

Section 8

Working with multiple colours

An essential skill required when making computer cut vinyl signs, is the ability to produce designs made up from multiple colours.

Many logos, lettering and graphics consist of more than one colour. A typical example would be a piece of lettering with a drop shadow effect.

This chapter will now describe the basic principle behind creating a drop shadow effect and realising this as an actual sign. This section will demonstrate the process using Corel draw, but it is important to realise than any vector drawing package can achieve the same effect. Indeed, many dedicated sign programs contain special features and tools that make this process even easier than the way it is done in the process described next

The first step is to design the lettering

In this example we have typed the message "Shadow" and coloured this yellow using the softwares paint pallete.

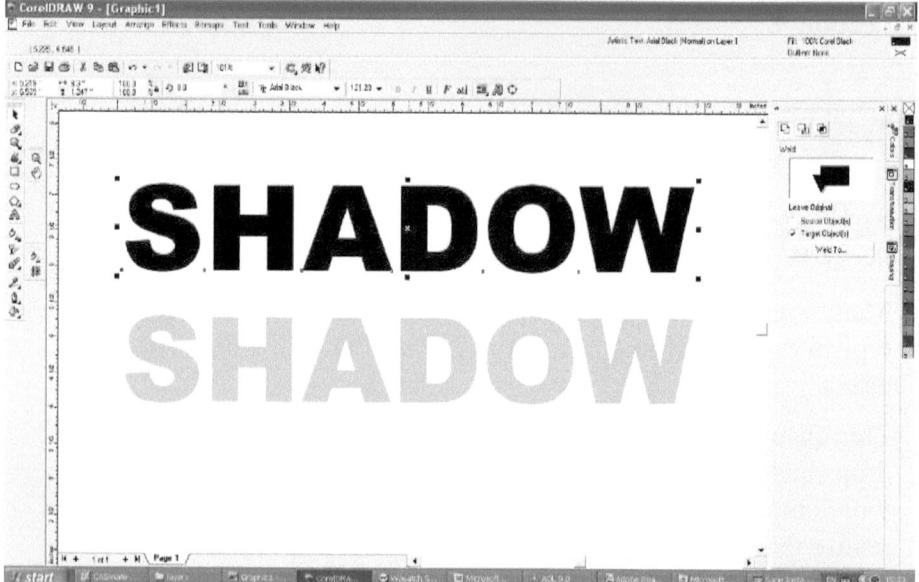

Next we must make a copy of the lettering and colour this a different colour (e.g. black).

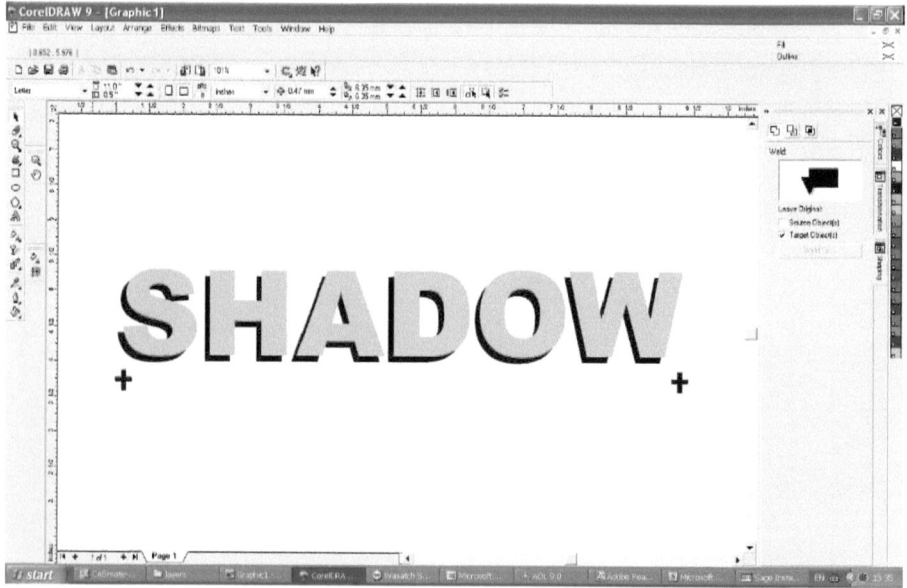

Now the black lettering is simply placed behind the yellow lettering to create the shadow effect shown above. At this stage a couple of registration markers are added to the design. Most dedicated sign software design packages will have a feature to automatically generate registration marks, however, if using a drawing package such as Corel these markers have to be manually drawn. This can be achieved quite simply by drawing two rectangle in the shape of a cross as shown.

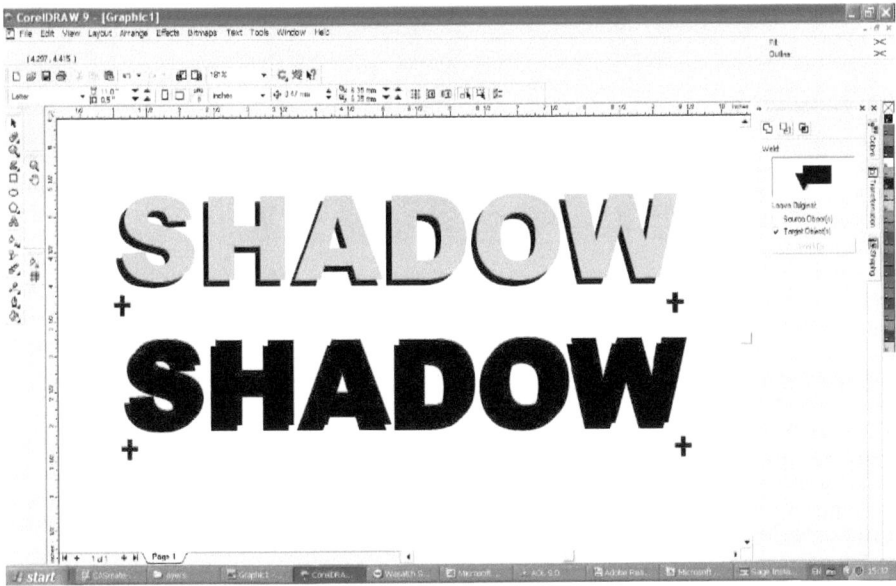

The design is now duplicated and coloured black as shown on the lower half of the screen grab shown above.

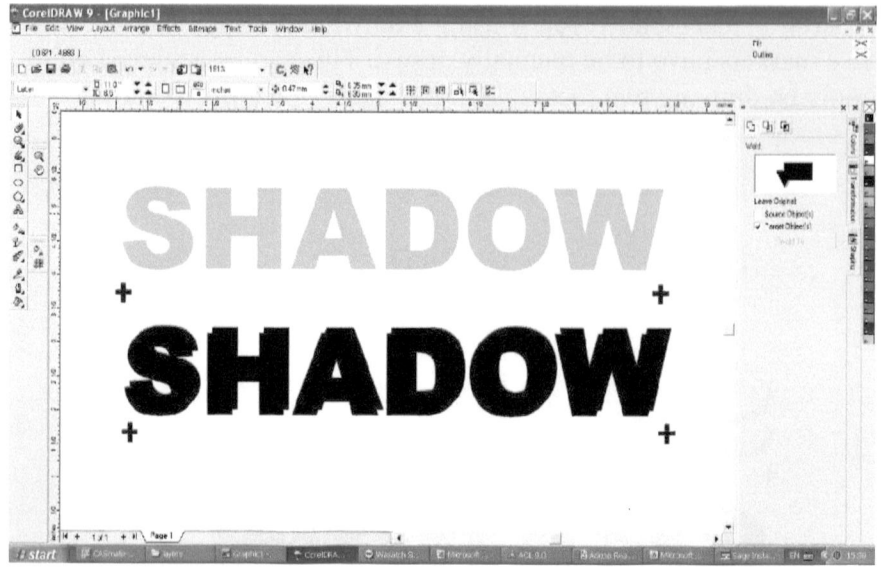

Now the black lettering underneath the yellow lettering (on the top half of the illustration) can be deleted. Next the black lettering as shown on the bottom half of the image is "welded" to produce a combined object which can be cut from vinyl. Welding features vary from design software to design software. These methods are a very powerful tool for the vinyl signmaker as they effectively reduce the number of cut paths in the designs to allow the vinyl to be cut without any excess lines to interfere with the design.

Above – Prior to carrying out a weld operation

Above – After weld operation

To try and explain this more clearly the previous two images show the unpainted version of the earlier illustration. As you can see, the lower section consists of both the original lettering and the copy of the original lettering that was placed underneath to create the drop shadow effect. After the "weld combine" operation has been carried out, the lower section consists of just one set of combined lettering.

In the un welded version you can see two sets of lettering placed one on top of the other (albeit slightly offset – thus creating the appearance of the drop shadow). However, if you tried to cut this before carrying out this operation we would have produced a number of unnecessary cut paths which would have cut extra lines into the vinyl and ruined the cutting process.

Having created separate component colours making up the design (each complete with its own set of registration markers) it is a simple process to first load the yellow vinyl in to the cutter and cut the yellow aspect of the design. Then change vinyl to black and cut the black part.

The image shown above shows the cut vinyl which has now been weeded ready for taping and applying to the substrate. Note that the yellow lettering has yellow crosses and the black lettering has black crosses. These "registration marks" will be used next to align the two layers and produce the resulting image.

Here we see the two colours taped and ready to apply.

The first colour to be applied to the substrate is black – this is the lower layer of the design.

Next the top layer is applied consisting of the yellow lettering. The registration marks (crosses) are used to visually align the top layer in its correct position above the lower layer.

On removing the application tape, you can see the overall effect.

The final step is to remove the registration marks as these were only used for alignment. These are simply removed from the substrate after the vinyl has just been applied.

The principles demonstrated are the same whatever drawing package you decide to use. Any number of colours can be utilised to create stunning effects and designs in cut vinyl. The use of registration markers ensures the colours are orientated correctly when the vinyl layers are finally applied to the backing material making up the sign.

Section 9 - Fitting signs using Sign Trim

Sign trim is mainly used for fitting signs made from PVC or acrylic material. It serves a number of purposes:-

1/ To allow sign panels to be fitted to a building without any visible fixings.
2/ To allow the sign panel to expand and contract in varying temperatures without warping.
3/ To provide a framing system and finished appearance to the sign.

Sign trim is produced by extruding aluminium through a suitable die. The die determines the profile of the extrusion and a range of profiles are available from a number of different manufacturers. All sign trim extrusions are used in the same way to allow the sign panel to hang inside the frame with space to expand and contract.

Above – cross sectional view of a typical sign extrusion

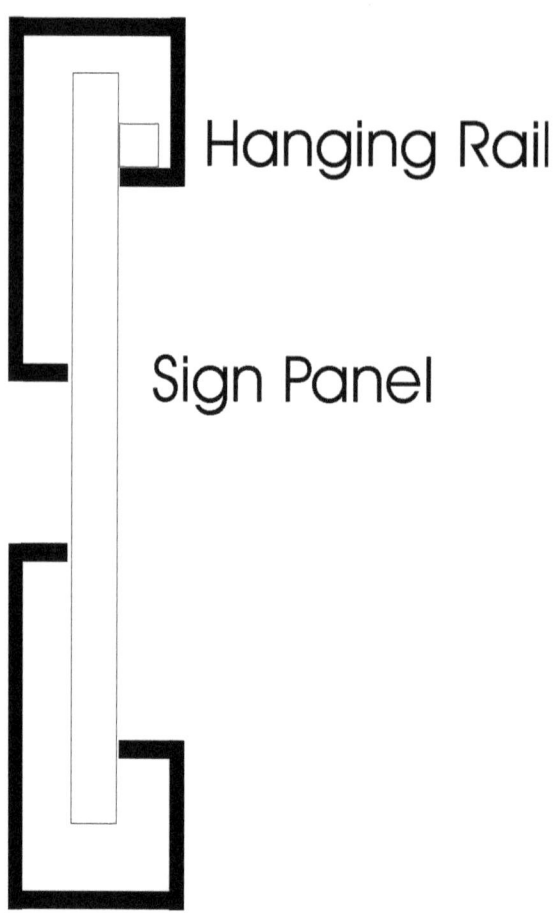

In this diagram you can see how the sign panel hangs from the top lip of the extrusion. The sign panel itself has a hanging rail attached to the front. This allows the sign panel to expand in all directions - top/bottom – left/right..

The first step to making a sign trim frame is to take an extrusion and mitre the corners. This can be done using an electrical mitre saw (or for the very energetic using a hand mitre saw).

Above – Electric mitre saw

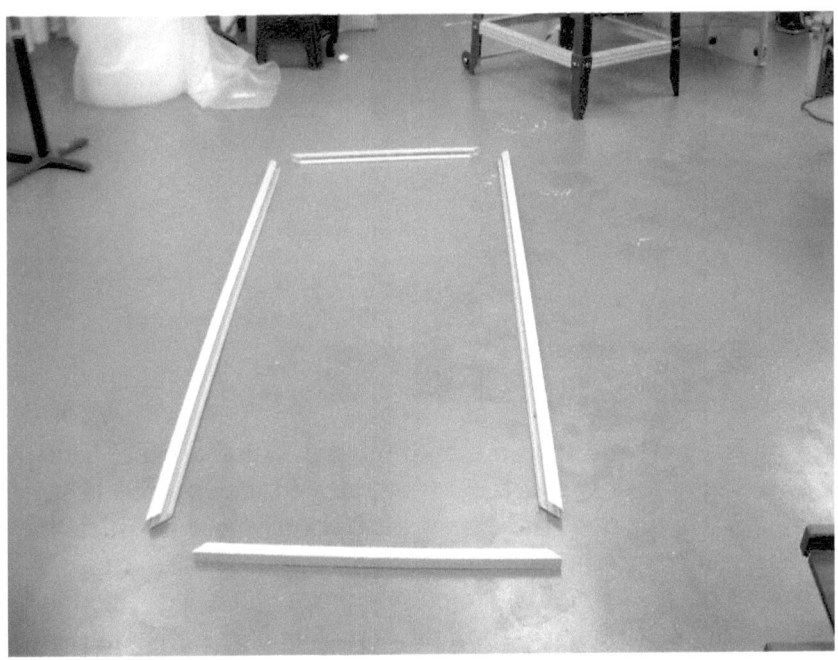

The four sections making up the sign frame are cut to length using the mitre saw ensuring a 45 degree angle cut at each end of the extrusion.

The extrusions are then joined together to form a rectangular shaped frame using suitable corner joining pieces.

Different manufacturers use different types of corner joint. The most basic type being a simple aluminium extrusion bent at 90 degrees. These are fitted into the ends of each length to allow the corners to align together at 90 degrees. The method I am using here consists of "push in" connectors. These have a serrated edge that allows it to be gently hammered into the end of the extrusion. The serrations prevent the joint from pulling back out. There are two types of connector used here. One has serrations to both ends which means that once in place the fitting is permanent. The other type is permanent on one side only to allow the extrusion to be pulled away again later.

Here you can see two extrusions both fitted with corner pieces. On the left we have the removable corner (non serrated with a screw hole in the middle). On the right is the permanent corner piece in which the serrations can be clearly seen on the exposed end. These extrusions now are connected by gently hammering the serrated edge into the corresponding extrusions to form the complete frame. The non permanent joint is simply pushed into place ready to be removed again later.

Above - The completed frame.

The completed frame can be attached to the building simply by fastening the frame along the top and bottom extrusions. However, in some cases it may be necessary to rivet additional strips to the back of the frame to provide additional mounting points.

This particular sign is going on a building which has horizontal corrugations, I have therefore elected to rivet strips of aluminum/polyethylene composite (e.g. Dibond) to the back of the frame to provide additional support.

Here you can see some of the strips of Dibond attached to the back of the frame.

Next a hanging rail is attached to the front of the sign panel. In this example the sign has been made using a 5mm gloss foam PVC board onto which the finished cut vinyl design has been applied. The hanging rail is made from off cuts of the 5mm foam board cut down into thin strips.

The hanging rail is attached to the front of the sign panel using a double sided tape. For extra security, the hanging rail is also held in place using screws.

The corners of the sign panel also need to be trimmed as shown to allow clearance between the sign panel itself and the corner jointing pieces once the panel has been fitted into the frame.

Above – sign panel shown with hanging rail attached and "cut outs" in the corner.

Next the complete frame is attached to the building using suitable fixings. In this example I have used self drilling cladding screws to attach the frame to the cladding of the building.

The picture below shows one of the fixings in place in the corner of a similar frame. Note that once the panel has been fitted the fixings will then be hidden from view.

Next you can see one of the sign panels being inserted into the end of the sign frame. The hanging rail at the top of the panel engages with the lower lip of the top extrusion and the panel slides into the frame from the left hand side.

Above – the first panel making up the sign having been slid partially into place.

The first panel is pushed along to the right of the frame, and the right hand edge of the panel fits in place in the right hand extrusion making up the frame.

Next the second panel is slid into the frame from the left hand side..

At this stage, I fasten a series of tongues to the back of each panel where the two halves of the sign will meet up. These are made from scrap PVC and are attached to the back of the panels using double sided tape. The "tongues" are staggered so that when the two panels are brought together, they will interlock holding them in place together (fore and aft). This helps to prevent the wind from getting behind the join and potentially blowing one of the panels out of the frame during stormy conditions.

In the next picture you can see the two panels (prior to closing together) showing the staggered "tongues" (sometimes called interlocking "fingers") attached to the back of each panel.

Finally, with the two panels closed up, the end piece is pushed back onto the frame and held in place using screws through the extrusion.

The completed sign.

Section 10 - Vehicle signs

Designing and applying vehicle liveries is one of my favourite types of sign.

Why do I enjoy this aspect of sign making so much? I think there are many reasons.

First and foremost I like to see the transformation of an ordinary van that arrives blank first thing in the morning and departs later the same day with eye catching signs advertising the owners business.

Secondly, I can do all of the work, from designing, to producing the vinyl graphics, to finally fitting all on my own premises without the need to go on site. This means I am in my own place ready to take any phone calls and enquiries that may come in while I am working. It's not weather dependant either. I don't have to rely on good weather in order to carry out my work unless of course it's a very large vehicle too tall to fit under the roller shutter at the entrance to our premises.

Finally it's well paid work that tends to bring in a lot of repeat business. Often there is no need to re-design when an existing customer buys a new van. They normally want their existing design adapted to suit the new vehicle.

Any serious sign maker should invest in a set of up to date vehicle outlines. These consist of scaled or full sized drawings of commercial vehicles and a range of other vehicles such as cars. These libraries can be bought from specialist suppliers that concentrate on bringing out new outlines as and when new commercial vehicles are introduced. These libraries are designed to be used in a wide range of vector drawing packages. In most cases when imported into your regular sign design software they appear as full size editable diagrams of the vehicle in question. They can then be coloured to match the clients actual van and the design is then drawn on top of the outline.

Vehicle Preparation – in most cases the only preparation required before applying vinyl graphics to a vehicle is a good wash and dry. Occasionally residual glues may be left on a vehicle when old lettering has been removed. These glues can be removed using tar removing cleaners such as "Autoglym" tar remover, but many other commercial cleaning solvents exist to remove these glues.

Occasionally you may be asked to remove all of the old vinyl lettering on a vehicle before re-signing with the new livery. Make sure you charge enough for your time if undertaking this work. Removal of old vinyl lettering is not difficult but can be very time consuming. It is often difficult to guess how long it would take to remove existing lettering as there are many variables. Sometimes the vinyl comes off cleanly leaving very little residue. But equally, removing lettering can turn into a nightmare if the vinyl is very brittle and leaves behind a lot of glue. I usually avoid offering a fixed price up front to carry out this type of work. I prefer to quote an hourly rate and explain that it is difficult to predict how long it might take to remove old vinyl. Often the client will elect to remove old signs themselves.

The best way to remove old vinyl is to apply heat. Either use a hair dryer or hot air gun. My favourite method is to use a wall paper stripper. This puts plenty of heat in the form of steam onto the bodywork and vinyl surface. This allows you to peel away the vinyl in one piece usually leaving little or no glue residue. Very small lettering can be quickly removed this way when a wall paper stripper is used in conjunction with a plastic squeegee blade such as that used for applying vinyl.

So how do we go about creating and applying a van livery?

First the design for the vehicle is drawn up on a computer

This consists of importing a vehicle outline into the computers memory. On the rare occasion that we do not have an outline for a particular vehicle, we can take a digital picture of the actual van and import this into the design software instead. Then by taking some critical measurements such as the vehicles wheel base and width, these photographs can be scaled to actual size in the design software.

The lettering and graphics are then drawn onto the outline (or digital picture).

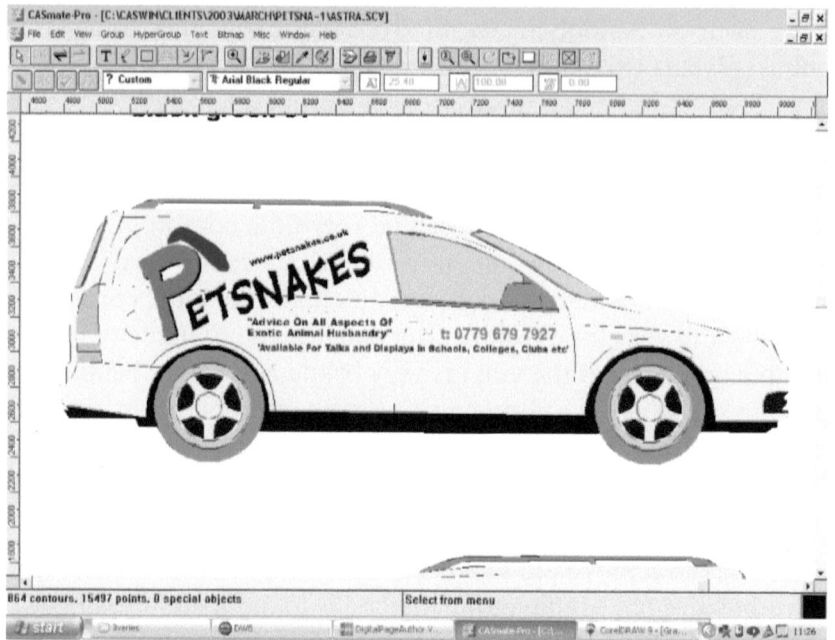

The final layout can then be printed out or sent by email to be approved by the customer.

Above - design work in progress

The individual components of the layout are sent to the plotter which cuts out the shapes of all of the lettering and graphics in the design.

Here you can see the green components of this layout being cut into the vinyl material

Once cut - the excess vinyl is removed leaving behind individual lettering and graphical shapes on the backing paper.

Here you can see the lettering being prepared ready for taping and transfering to the vehicle bodywork

Above you can see the pre-spaced lettering has been lifted off the backing paper using a transfer tape. This is then placed in position on the bodywork and stuck on by applying pressure over the transfer paper with an applicator.

The transfer tape is then carefully peeled away to leave all of the lettering and graphics in place on the bodywork.

This particular design also features a rendered image (photo quality) of a snake.

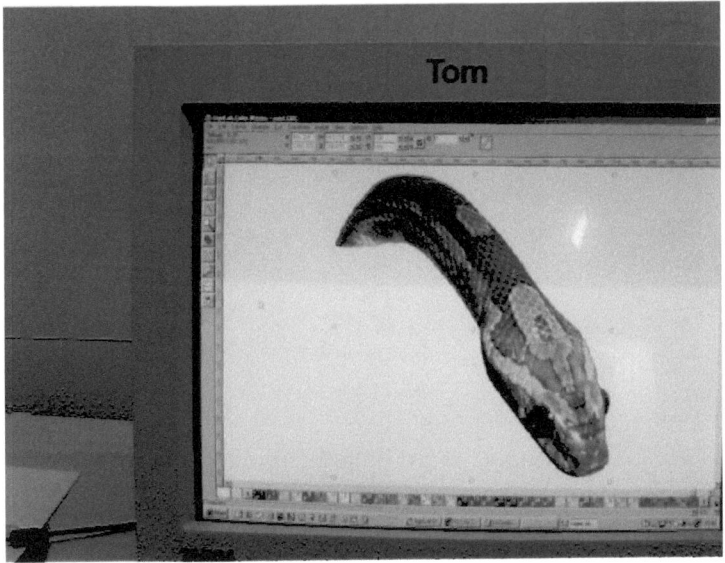

The photograph is first edited on the computer and made ready to be sent out to a dedicated printing and cutting device

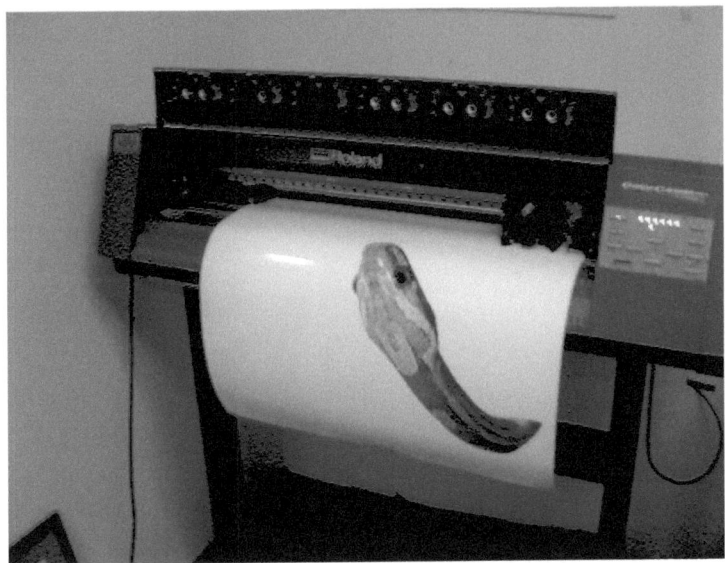

Here you can see the image of the snake being printed on a Roland Colorcamm. This device uses Thermal Transfer technology to produce an outdoor durable print for inclusion on a sign.

Above is the printed image of the snake cut out and ready for applying to the vehicle. Also shown is the green vinyl shape making up the letter "P"

Below - the letter "P" is added to the existing black lettering and finally the picture of the snake is also applied to the bodywork

The completed van

Whenever a client comes to collect a vehicle that has just been signed I always provide him or her with a printout of the following:-

"CARING FOR YOUR VEHICLE GRAPHICS"

Vehicle signs are one of the most cost effective ways to advertise your business.

To ensure you get the best possible service from the signs that have just been applied to this vehicle, please bear the following points in mind:-

Any small bubbles visible in freshly applied vinyl graphics will disappear in a day or two – this is quite normal.

Graphics should not normally be washed for about a week after application (adhesives need time to flow to build a stronger bond with the surface).

Standard car washes may then be safely used, but care should be taken with high pressure wands or washers. Spray pressure must not be more than 1,500 Pounds of water per square inch, and

temperatures should be no higher than 180 degrees F (64.5 C). When these washes are used, the nozzle should be kept at least a foot away from the vehicle and at a perpendicular angle.

If at some point in the future you wish to remove these graphics this can be achieved as follows:-

Gently heat with a hair drier (this helps to soften the vinyl and the glue), it will then be possible to carefully peel away the vinyl in one piece. Any remaining marks or glue can then be removed using a suitable solvent such as white spirit or"Autoglym" tar and adhesive remover."

Giving your customer this printout serves a number of functions

1/ - It offers advice and guidance on caring for vehicle graphics

2/ - It reminds the client that what he is paying for is a very effective means of advertising

3/ - Finally, it shows the customer that you actually care.

Section 11 - Flat cut lettering signs

Flat cut lettering signs are made by cutting out individual shapes from a range of sheet materials such as Acrylic and Dibond. These component parts are then fitted to a surface such as a shop fascia using "stand off" locators.

The end result is a set of letters fastened directly to the buildings brickwork or wooden fascia.

The first step in the process is to design the sign. This involves drawing up the shape of the shop front to which the individual letters will be attached. This is drawn up full size based on critical measurements taken on site during the initial survey. Nowadays, it is just as easy to take a digital picture of the shop front and scale this to "actual size" in your regular design software.

Superimposed on the drawing or photograph is the actual design. In this instance a font called Avant Garde will be used.

The layout is then either printed off or emailed to the client for approval.

Above – design work in progress

Once the layout has been approved the font being used is converted to curves – usually by invoking the "convert to curves" function of the software, or by carrying out a simple "weld" operation . The resultant graphic is then exported as an .eps or .ai at actual size from the design software.

Above - The lettering layout set out actual size ready to be exported as an .eps or .ai file

The exported file containing the information required to cut the shapes is then sent off to a specialist supplier of flat cut lettering. These suppliers use the .eps or .ai file to drive a CNC router to cut the shapes into the sheet material specified.

In this example, we will be using 3mm Butler Dibond material which has a brushed Aluminium finish. The supplier will also fix stand off locators to the rear of each component letter and produce the paper template required to set out the design on the fascia and drill holes to accept the letterings female locators.

Alternatively, the signmaker can use his plotter to cut vinyl lettering at actual size which is then applied to the sheet material to be cut out by hand using a fret saw.

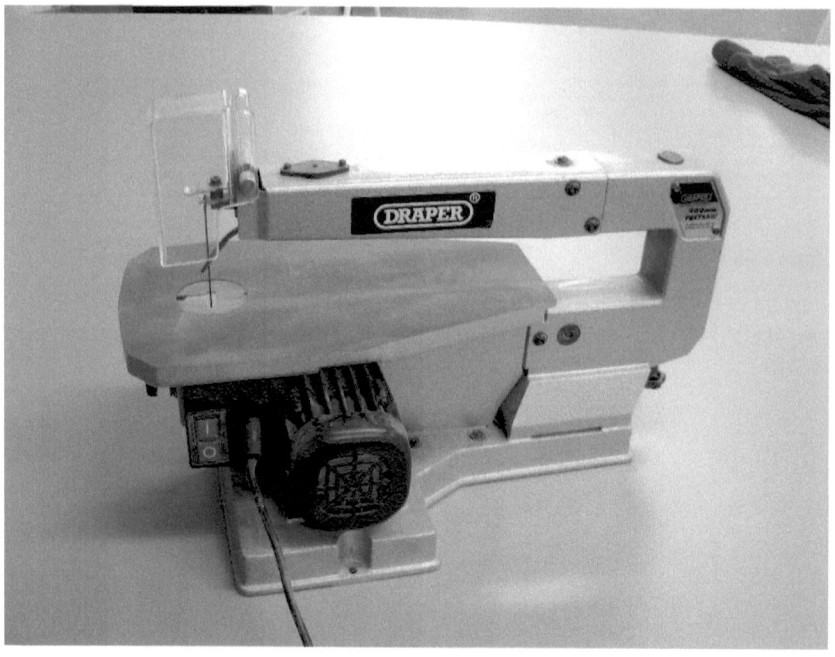

Above – example of electric powered fretsaw (however, even using an electrical powered fretsaw such as this is a very time consuming method for creating individual flat cut letters).

The signmaker then also needs to make up his own template by using his plotter fitted with a pen or pencil to draw the design out at actual size on a sheet of paper. Next male locators are glued to the back of each letter which is then pressed down on top of it's corresponding outline on the paper template. By doing this impressions are made on the paper template which are then clearly defined using a pen to mark crosses at the central point of every locator on every letter. These marks will be used later to drill holes in the correct position on the building when fitting the component parts.

My personal opinion is that it is no longer cost effective to produce your own shapes by hand. Modern CNC routers produce this much quicker and more accurately. The time saved is substantial and easily justifies the extra cost in "buying in".

When pricing these jobs I usually send off the .eps file to my supplier to obtain a quotation to supply all of the lettering. The price quoted is then subject to our normal mark up, then our design fee and installation costs are added to produce the quotation that is sent to the client.

Here you can see the set of flat cut lettering that has just arrived back from the supplier. Using the template I sent them, they have produced all of the shapes in Butler Dibond (Brushed aluminium). This has been set out on top of the paper template that they also supplied in order to check all the parts are there and in good order before setting off on site to carry out the install.

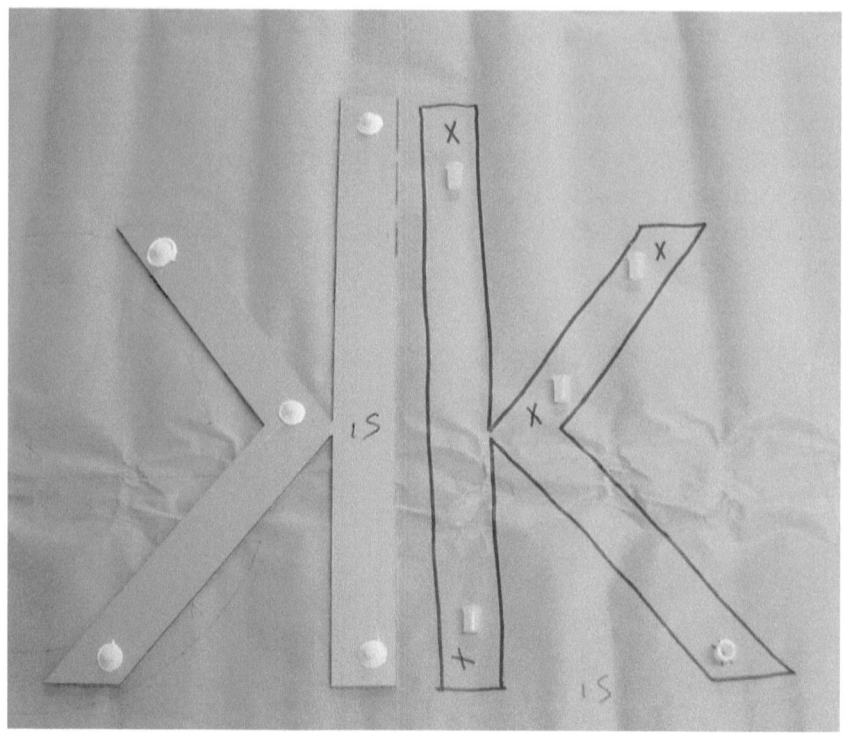

This is a close up of the back of the letter "k". Here you can see the male locators glued onto the back. On the right hand side is the outline drawn out on the paper template. The positions of all the locators are marked with an "x" to allow us to see where to drill the holes where the female locators (also shown – white plastic cups) are to be fitted onto the shop front fascia.

Above – Paper template in position

The first stage in the installation process is to stick the paper template in place on the building. I use "Duct Tape" (sometimes known as Duck Tape) to do this. This ensures the template remains in position while a series of holes are drilled to allow the female locators to be fitted in place. In this example the design will be centered above the doorway and slightly above centre top to bottom. All the shapes of the letters are drawn out on the template along with the crosses that indicate where the holes should be drilled. (Unfortunately, this is too faint to be visible in the photograph).

Installation of female locators:-

Here you can see a number of locators fixed in position on the fascia ready to accept the male connectors glued to the back of the individual dibond letters. I have used a felt tip pen to highlight the shape of the letter "k" purely for illustrative purposes. All the other shapes are also drawn out on the template but are to faint to be apparent in this series of photographs.

The locators are fitted using wall plugs and screws (having first drilled a series of holes in the positions marked on the paper template).

The paper template is then torn away revealing the building brickwork complete with the series of accurately spaced and aligned locators that the letters can plug onto.

In this picture the first few letters have now been fitted (to the right you can see the rest of the work in progress). The rest of the paper template is still in place to allow the locators for the rest of the design to be fitted.

Above - Installation work in progress.
Below – the completed installation.

Finally – all of the locators have been fitted and the rest of the paper template removed before plugging the rest of the flat cut letters in place.

Below – another view of the completed installation

As you can see – this type of sign is very effective and is usually popular in areas that have strict planning rules such as listed buildings.

No specialist tools are required over and above the software already in use for a typical vinyl sign business. All of the design is done using normal vector drawn graphics and the resultant design (.eps file) is also the software tool used by the specialist flat cut lettering supplier to produce the component parts.

Section 12 - Basic principles of good sign layout

The late Mike Stevens wrote a book called "Mastering Layout" which is generally regarded as the leading authority for students of good sign design and layout. Mike Stevens believed that good layout and design skills were not an inherent gift, but were skills that could be easily taught. In his book he describes simple rules and formulas that when followed would always ensure eye catching layouts would be produced.

Natural Layout:-

One of the fundamental styles he taught he christened "natural layout".

In natural layout we have three distinct groups. The main message (foreground), the secondary message (middleground) and the tertiary message (background).

The general rule is that for a sign to work well there should be no more than three distinct groups competing for attention. Furthermore, these distinct groups should be prioritised (foreground, middleground and background). If no priorities are given, then all three groups end up competing with each other for attention resulting in a messy looking sign which has no flow or eye appeal.

In this example we have three groups all of similar priority all competing for attention. The result is dull and uninteresting. Further more, no consideration has been given to the margin space surrounding the groups.

Example of "Natural Layout"

In this example we have set out the sign following the rules and formula for natural layout. We have a main message (the foreground). This is in the centre of the sign just above the middle height and is the main focus. The lettering here should be bolder and larger than anywhere else on the layout. Above this we have the secondary message set in the middle distance (middle ground). Underneath the main message we have the tertiary message set in the background (this is the smallest group).

Think of the sign as a three dimensional object with the foreground message right in front and the middle ground and background messages set out further and further away from the viewer.

The other vitally important aspect of natural layout is the importance of the margin spaces surrounding the messages. The outer margin space should be set out in the proportions as shown. Note also that the spaces between the groups of messages should never be larger than the margin space surrounding all three groups as a whole.

The importance of margin spaces should never be under estimated. Mike Stevens called this "Negative Space". A popular misconception amongst the layman is to make the lettering as big as possible to increase its impact. This is wrong! Maximum impact will only ever be achieved when the correct margin spaces are employed.

Now let's look at a fictional example to see how this could be interpreted as a sign that follows Mike Stevens natural layout rules and Formula.

Let's say we have to make a sign for the fictional company "Joe Bloggs Plumbing Services". First we must prioritise the copy.

In this example I would say the main message is "Plumbing" (The guy is a Plumber – and this is the main message he must tell the world if the sign is to work as an effective advertisement for his business). The secondary message is "Joe Bloggs" (His name). Some may argue that Joe Bloggs should be the main message but I would disagree. Who cares what his real name is? All we really want to know is the type of business he runs which is "Plumbing". Finally, the tertiary message is "Services" – this is just an appendum to the name he calls his business.

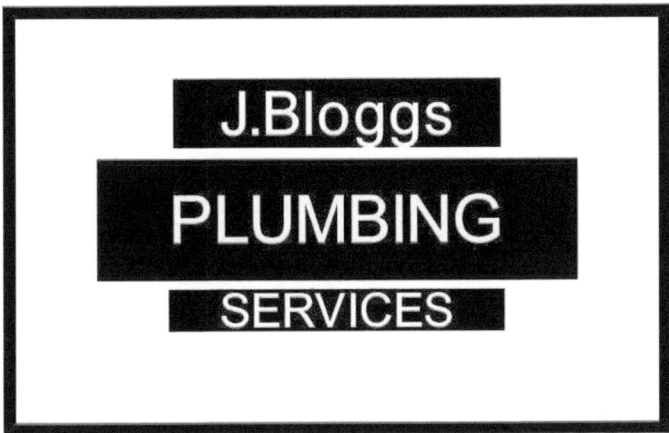

Here we see "J Bloggs Plumbing Services" set out as three separate groups all following the natural layout formula. This is our starting point.

Note that in this particular example each message consists of only one word, however this need not always be the case.

These same rules apply equally to groups containing more than one word. (See the "Private Property" example sign at the end of this chapter).

Now we substitute the main message with the intended style of lettering. For the main message I usually use a thick heavy bold font that is easy to read (it's the main message after all – so let's make it easy to understand). In this example I have used a font called "Eurostar Black" but any easily read heavy bold font (such as Arial Black etc.) would have a similar effect.

Now we must turn our attention to the secondary message. In this case "J. Bloggs". Now, as this is a persons name, I usually like to use a scripted style of font (to give it the appearance of a persons signature). Legibility in this case is not so important as in the main message so I have used one of my favourite scripted fonts called "Rapier". However, there are many beautiful scripted fonts available that can be used to the same effect.

Next we turn to the tertiary message "Services". We need to choose a font that does not compete as much for attention as the main message font and the scripted font. It's not usually a good idea to use too many fonts in a single design, so in this instance I have chosen to use the regular version of the bold font used for the main message. In this case Eurostyle Regular.

Another thing to note is that I have chosen uppercase lettering for "Plumbing" and "services". This is done deliberately to give a regular edge to the top of each group (rather than a jagged edge which would be the case if using lower case lettering). This allows the lettering above to sit over an even margin space which is more pleasing to the eye.

Finally, the finished product. In this instance I have added a couple of lines above and below the main message to increase its importance in the design. Note that where the "down legs" of the scripted lettering have imposed upon the top line I have created breaks in the line to improve the legibility of the lettering above.

The design is now complete and ready for final bells and whistles. At this stage we may choose to add colours and effects such as shadows. However, I have always believed that before adding colour and shadow effects, it is important to get the basic layout right.

In this example we have used exactly the same layout rules but substituted different fonts with similar line value (weight) in their corresponding message groups. The design now takes on a different appearance but still has eye appeal due to the fact that natural layout rules have been followed.

Try it for yourself. You can even use the same fonts if you wish but it's usually better to vary the fonts used in different designs. However, even when the same fonts are used it is surprising how different each design looks when a different set of messages is being conveyed.

The same principles can be applied time and time again to produce layouts that are always pleasing to the eye – and yet (with different messages and fonts being used) will always look unique and individual.

Do Not Enter

PRIVATE PROPERTY

Trespassers will be prosecuted

Even a simple warning notice can be made to look more interesting when the principles of natural layout are employed in the design.

(Note that in the last example there are three groups of messages all with different priorities. Each group contains more than one word - not just single words).

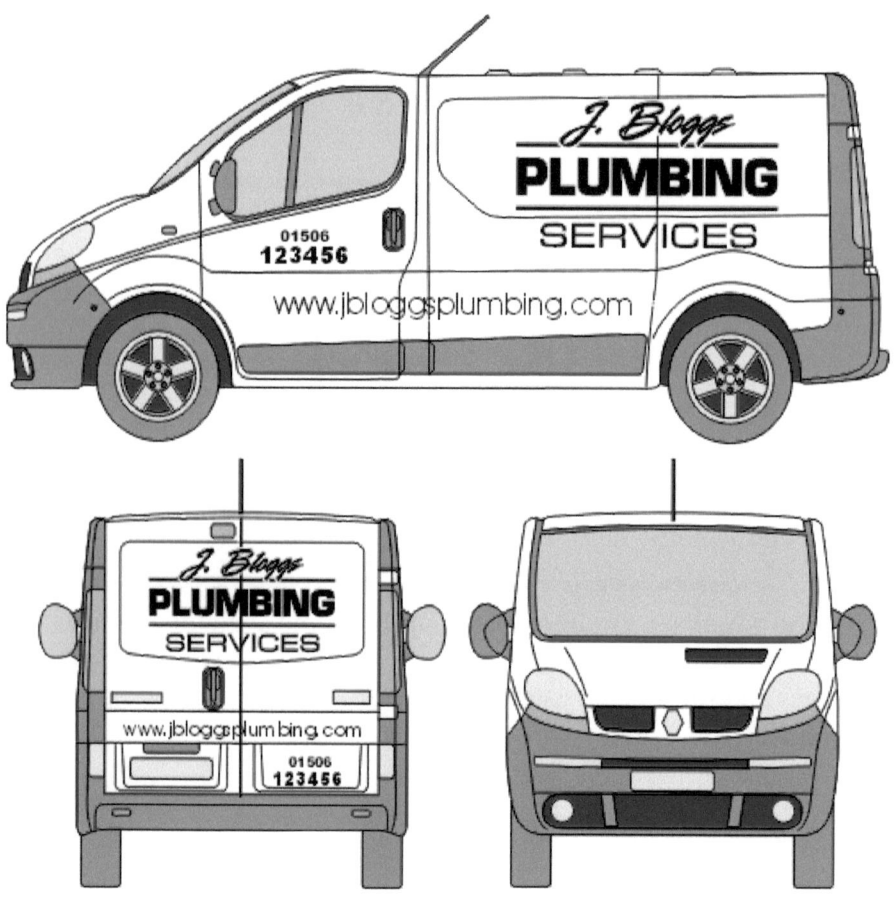

Add a simple email address and a telephone number and already you have the makings of a professional looking vehicle livery

Section 13 - How to price your work

For the new business owner, one of the most difficult aspects of running a sign business is pricing.

Getting it wrong can cause all sorts of problems. If your prices are too high you may find you spend all your time quoting work to no avail. All the work is going elsewhere (and you may not get the chance to quote again in future if you get a reputation for being too expensive).

Equally as bad (and possibly an even bigger problem) is under pricing your work. The signmaker that under prices his jobs may find himself extremely busy - but at the end of the year (having paid all of his business overhead expenses) making very little profit!! I cannot emphasise enough the importance of having proper control over your pricing.

Calculating your hourly rate.

The crucial element for pricing work in any company that provides a service is the hourly rate. It is essential to get this part right if you hope to have proper control over your business. Before looking at the hourly rate charged by your competitors, I suggest you carry out the following exercise:-

First you need to calculate your overheads. These are your fixed costs. Items such as rent, rates, advertising and any wages paid to employees etc. (all the expenses a small business must pay simply to exist and before it can make any profit). It should not include your variable costs such as the materials used in manufacturing signs etc.

Now decide how much you need to earn to make this enterprise worthwhile.

Finally, work out how many hours a year you and any employees you have can expect to be usefully employed producing and installing signs. Remember to take into account holidays, and the fact that you will not spend all of your time actually producing and installing signs. You will also need to allow time for visiting clients, producing quotations, and dealing with all the other aspects of running your own small company.

To help you understand how to calculate an hourly rate, let's look at a practical example:-

Let's assume you are a sole trader with overheads of say £20,000 a year (i.e. your fixed costs).

Now let's assume you have decided that in order to make this business worthwhile, you wish to pay yourself £25,000 a year.

Therefore, using these figures as an example - in total you need to charge £45,000 a year for your labour.

Now assuming you work 48 weeks a year, 5 days a week, 5 hours a day producing signs (remember the rest of the time you will be doing other work that will not be generating income - hence the 5 hours a day). Note that in this example of a sole trader, there are no additional employees that would be making signs

Using these example figures - the total number of hours spent actually producing signs in a year would be :-

48 x 5 x 5 = 1200

Therefore - in order to generate an income of £45,000 - your hourly rate needs to be 45,000/1200 = £37.50 per hour

Now that you have calculated your hourly rate, you must keep it fixed in your mind at all times when pricing and carrying out work. In future, when producing, installing or manufacturing signs, do a mental calculation to check whether or not you are charging enough for each job you are doing. You must target to meet your overheads and also to give yourself a decent profit. When doing any sign related work I am constantly aware of my hourly rate and I continuously check to see if I am earning enough on any job I do.

You also need to compare your rate with those charged by your competitors. Don't be tempted to undercut - and if you are up against tough competition, you may find you have to trim your rate to remain competitive. However, all is not lost - there is another way your business generates profit. This is the "mark up" on the materials you use when you produce your signs

There are a number of ways that sign makers price their signs, here is a brief description of some of the most common methods:-

(1) A popular method is to measure the individual letter heights of all of the lettering used in a sign. The sign maker has a set rate for individual letters of different heights and uses these rates to calculate a price. This method harks back to the days of the sign writer who would charge according to the size and number of letters making up the sign he was painting. The main disadvantages of this method are that it can be quite time consuming to calculate the price of a sign - and this price will require changing every time the copy of the sign changes.

(2) Another popular method is to apply a multiple of the materials cost to produce the sign. In other words, the sign maker calculates the cost (to him) to produce a sign based on the materials used - and multiplies this by some factor (e.g 4 to 10) to arrive at the final price. The main disadvantage here is that no account is taken of the time required to produce the sign. With the first method (Individual letter heights) there is at least some semblance of taking into account the time required to make the sign based on the amount of lettering involved. On the plus side, an advantage of this second method is that it is relatively quick and easy to calculate a selling price.

(3) Many sign makers like to use a set of tables to arrive at prices based on the size of a sign. This is similar to using the materials cost method (2) - but is a bit more sophisticated in that a smaller sign can be priced to be proportionately more expensive than a large sign. This reflects well on the fact that a small sign can take almost as long to make as a large sign.

Paul Hughes an established sign maker recently published a booklet called the sign pricing guide which contains a series of look up tables for various sizes and types of signs. This can be obtained by registering on his website www.priceitsignguide.com

(4) An ideal method is to use your hourly rate and add to this the materials cost to produce your sign. Normally the materials cost would also be subject to a mark up of say 1.5 to 3 times of the cost to you the sign maker. This method is perhaps one of the fairest methods of pricing - but can be quite time consuming and it is often difficult to give a price to the customer prior to beginning work.

(5) My preferred method:- A spreadsheet can be constructed that combines many of the principles already discussed for pricing signs. The spreadsheet we have devised uses a combination of materials costs and their mark up, size of sign, look up tables, numbers of colours

used and hourly rates. The main advantage of this method is that (although highly sophisticated and taking into account all of the above) it is a very quick method of pricing. It's also very consistent.

Charging based on perceived value.

There is a strong case for arguing that you should price work according to what the market will bear. In other words, not as a result of calculating your hourly rate plus materials costs and mark up, but on the basis of what value the signs you produce are worth to the client.

This approach removes the ceiling you will have placed on your potential earnings when adopting a fixed hourly rate. Using this method allows you to potentially make much higher profits.

From the customers point of view it does not matter how long a job takes – their real concern is the end result. Thus if the work you produce can be done very quickly and economically, but is very eye catching and looks expensive – then you should charge a higher price for it.

Also, if the signs you produce are bringing in more business for your customer then they have a higher perceived value than signs that merely instruct (such as warning signs and instructional signs). Signs that advertise a business are worth more than the equivalent sign that merely conveys instructional information.

For example, I always remind our customers when we are asked for a price to sign a van, that his van works as an advertising medium for his business. When discussing typical example prices for different types of vans I often remind them that the van will be advertising the business for as long as the van is in service. In most cases this will be three to five years and when looked at from this perspective a £200 price tag for a set of van signs begins to look like exceptional value for money (advertise for five years at only £40 a year i.e. less than £1 a week for advertising). Using this approach will often sway the customer into making a buying decision and convince him that vehicle signs do indeed represent excellent value for money.

How do you put a value on a brilliant design? You probably can't – at the end of the day the value of a sign is as much as the buyer is prepared to pay. For signmakers that are particularly skilled in producing eye catching layouts there is potential to charge more.

In some cases, when quoting for work you are often going to be responsible for producing original designs. It's only fair and correct that you should be paid for the creative aspect of what you design. Many bread and butter type signs fall into the hourly rate and materials cost category, and rightly so. But when there is a unique design element required by the signmaker this is less easily quantified.

A new start business will not have a reputation for producing good work and original and eyecatching designs. But as the business builds and progresses over time you may expect to achieve a reputation for producing not only good quality work , but original and eyecatching designs also.

I would suggest that the new start business devoid of a reputation does not have the track record to demand high fees and should adopt the approach of pricing according to the hourly rate and materials mark up method described earlier. The more mature business however, should be looking to charge more on the basis of the perceived value his signs will bring to any customer.

In reality, most sign companies will use a combination of methods when pricing. Certain types of jobs lend themselves naturally to an hourly rate method (installation work for example, or basic signage such as health and safety information). Other jobs (such as a one off van livery – or an upmarket restaurant sign) are more about perceived value.

Other factors also come into play when pricing work, amongst these are the following factors:-

1/ How much do you want to do this job?

2/ How busy are you – do you need this work?

3/ Is the job full of hassles and complications?

4/ Is this a regular customer or a one off?

5/ Is this a prestigious job that will reflect well on you?

The above factors (and more) will influence the pricing of any job.

At this stage we seem to have moved away from pricing as a "hard and fast science following a set of rigid rules and guidelines" into being something more of a "black art".

My belief is that to be a successful sign business you need to constantly monitor your pricing and strategy according to the current market conditions and your own current set of circumstances. In many cases you need to follow the rule of pricing according to an hourly rate and mark up of materials, but equally, in certain circumstances, you should also be charging according to the perceived value that your signs will add to the buyers business.

At the very least, my advice is to never drop below your hourly rate when producing signs. Some may argue that (when quiet) some work is better than no work. I disagree with this point of view. If working for less than your hourly rate you are selling yourself short and in danger of failing as a business. If short of work, rather than take on low paid jobs, your time would be better spent marketing your enterprise and finding new customers.

Section 14 – Marketing your business

"Without customers you don't have a business"

The most essential element required to make any enterprise a success is customers. It doesn't matter how good your products or services are, without customers you do not have a viable business.

Signs are ubiquitous. So there is no denying the fact that if you can produce signs at a price that people will pay, and at a price which still allows you to make a profit – then you have the potential to form a profitable company.

Marketing is, in essence, the way in which you tell people about the products and service you offer.

One of the best pieces of advice I ever heard when setting up was:-

"It's a numbers game – If you tell enough people about what you do, you will get the work".

That piece of advice is certainly true.

You do not need any gimmicks, you do not even need to be any different in the products or services you offer than any other sign company. You just need to provide a service at least as good as (but preferably better than) your competitors.

So assuming you can make signs, and assuming you can make a profit selling these at a similar price to the signs your competitors are selling. If you can get the message across to enough people that you are offering a competitive sign making service, then you have the makings of a viable business.

Without a doubt – the best form of advertising is "word of mouth". Do a good job for someone and the chances are they will tell someone else. However, do a bad job and the chances are a dissatisfied customer will tell loads of people. So look after all your customers.

However, until such time as you have a wide customer base to pass on word of mouth recommendations you are going to have to work hard to get the word out about your company.

Cold Calling

Cold calling certainly works. There are always people looking to buy signs. This may not be uppermost in their mind or top of their list of priorities at all times but never the less they are out there.

Before we even started, I carried out market research to determine whether or not it would be a good idea to start this type of business in our locality.

I obtained a mailing list of companies in my area and began by contacting the owners or managers. I basically described to them my intention to start a sign making business and began by asking them for advice and was this a service they would ever be likely to use? It was surprising the number of people that I spoke to that were at that moment in time in the market to buy signs of some sort or another. In many cases I would contact a local trades man who would respond by saying "I have been thinking about getting my van sign written – is that something you can do"?

During my market research I came across a number of examples of companies and individuals that would have welcomed a quotation from me. This encouraged me to go ahead and actually set up the sign making service we were planning.

When we did finally launch the business I went back to all the people that had given me a positive response and in many cases my first professional jobs came about as a result of my pre-launch "market research".

Telephone Marketing

When we first started I found the quickest way to contact a lot of people was by telephone.

I bought a contact list of companies in my area from my local business advisory service (In Scotland this is called Small Business Gateway). This list provided me with telephone numbers and addresses. Alternatively you can obtain a copy of your local chamber of commerce members directory.

I started off by working through the list and phoning various companies asking to speak to the business owner or general manager (in many cases the owners name appeared on my contact list so I was able to ask for them by name). Often I found it was hard to get through to the main contact (receptionists are trained to filter calls) – when this happened, I would speak to the receptionist instead.

I began by explaining that I had started a sign making business and asked if this was something they would ever have a use for. Often the answer was yes and I would follow this up with a letter and leaflet. Often I would strike lucky and would be told they had a van to be signed or some other signage requirement and this would lead to me quoting for some work.

Spend an hour on the phone every day and I guarantee you will obtain a few genuine leads to follow up. I suggest you phone first or last thing in the day as this is the best time to get to speak to the business owner. Phoning allows you to speak to a lot more people in a given period of time than going around knocking on doors.

Back then (1996) I discovered that on average for every twelve calls I made, I would get one opportunity to quote for work. This was quite a high success rate especially when you consider that you can very easily make at least twelve phone calls of this type within an hour.

Without doubt – many people do not like cold calling – but it is still the most cost effective method of generating new leads and prospects.

On days when I went into work and had nothing to do – I could guarantee that within an hour or two of making phone calls I would have one or two sales leads lined up.

Networking – Business Clubs

Networking is something we all do whether we are aware of it or not. Some networking clubs are more "up front" than others. You can join your own local chambers of commerce and go along to any of their networking events armed with business cards. The purpose of these events is to meet with other people in your area in the hope that you can reciprocate business with them. At most events one or two individuals are given the opportunity to give a short presentation about their company. The idea is to mix with as many people and exchange information and business cards. Your local branch of the Federation of small business may also offer similar networking events. In addition to the organisations I have just mentioned there are also franchised networking clubs. In some cases these would involve business breakfasts where the members meet up perhaps once or twice a month at a hotel venue to network with other small businesses. These types of networking events are very upfront and positively encourage the members to recruit new members and to find leads for other members in their group.

A less formal type of networking exists when you mix with others socially or through sport. Always try to let people know about the type of work you do. You don't need to be in their face or pushy. But don't be afraid to use all the opportunities at your disposal to inform others about your business.

I recall a couple of years ago when my son played for a local football team. I used to take him to all the games in our van (which quite naturally is a good advert for the work we do). My son often complained and said "can't we take the car dad" and I always just half jokingly would say "no we're taking the van – it's good advertising". Lo and behold it finally paid off when one of the parents of another player in the team rang me up one day and asked me if I would be interested in quoting to supply signs to the company he worked for. He knew I made signs for a living simply because of the van (In all the times I spoke to him at the matches I never actually told him I was a sign maker, I didn't need to, he knew this from seeing me turn up to the games in our van). I have since provided thousands of pounds worth of signs for his employers.

Internet and websites

When we first started in 1996 the internet was just beginning to explode onto the scene. I remember in the late 1990's people saying that if you weren't an internet based company, pretty soon you would no longer be in business. I remember thinking "what a load of rubbish". I still think that is the case, but cannot deny that a website is a very cost effective means of promoting your company.

Eventually (around about 1999) I set up our own website.

There are two types of website. The first is an online brochure in which you use the site to describe your products and services. The second type is an on-line shop, where all your products are set out very much like a shop complete with shopping basket and check out.

The problem with offering signs for sale on a website is that in the main this is a bespoke service. Most signs are custom made for each individual customer. However, there are also certain types of signs that can be standardised, safety signs are a good example.

We have two sites. The main site is an online brochure designed to describe to the potential client the type of work we do. This works very well and I often receive new enquiries from people that have browsed the site before contacting me by phone. Many of their questions are already answered on the site. An online presence also helps enhance your businesses credibility, although nowadays people are becoming much more aware of how easy it can be to create a professional looking site that projects an image of a company much bigger and more established than it really is.

The second website is a safety sign site consisting of a full range of standard signs that can be browsed and subsequently ordered either by email, phone or fax. This site has contributed a great deal of turnover over the years that easily pays its running costs. Indeed, I have one particular customer that spends thousands of pounds on safety signs each year. This customer would never have found us if it hadn't been for our internet presence.

Email

One of the greatest advantages that have come about from the internet explosion is the use of email. Nowadays just about every person has email access and this makes communication very quick and easy. I now have a database of all my customers email addresses and often send a block email out to all of them informing them of any new developments or offers that may be of interest to them. In many ways, email has taken over from the use of the telephone and has many advantages.

Leaflets

Leaflets are an excellent way of creating awareness. A good leaflet describing your company is almost as important as having a business card. They can be sent out as part of a letter or pushed through the letterboxes of empty shops and factory units in the hope that the next tenant or owner to move into the property will find your leaflet of interest because (of course) he or she will be needing a new sign for their business when they move in.

Vehicle Signs

Without a doubt, vehicle signs are one of the best ways to advertise your business. I firmly believe this and tell this to all my customers when I do a van. Our own van is a showcase for the work we do. For this reason I like to keep it clean and looking fresh and up to date. After all, if a sign company doesn't have an effective vehicle livery, how can we expect to inspire our customers to believe we can produce a brilliant design for them.

I regularly get enquiries when I am out and about as a result of people seeing our van. I always keep business cards handy (on the dashboard) ready to give to any prospects who express an interest in the work we do.

My best ever result was in a single afternoon. I was out fitting a sign at a shop and was approached by three other shop owners in the same street, all asking me to provide them with a quotation for some sign work. All three enquiries ended up as sales.

Advertising

What can I say about advertising? Well it is expensive that's for sure, and not terribly well targeted in most cases. I believe all small businesses do need an advert in yellow pages. Not because we get a lot of work through this medium, but because I believe the majority of people use the Yellow Pages as a reference book. I do it too. Many existing customers who do not have your telephone number handy will normally pick up Yellow Pages in their first attempt to obtain your number. I do not get many new enquiries through this medium – We probably get more new enquiries as a result of potential customers seeing our van. However, I do believe we need to be in there.

I also believe sign making is predominantly a business to business service. Indeed, I do not think we get many quality enquiries from the general public. And (in any case) work carried out for the general public tends not to be of a repeat nature.

In our particular circumstances, we are on the very periphery of our local yellow pages. Perhaps this explains the lack of success we experience with this medium. From discussion with other established sign makers there seems to be a range of opinion of how successful advertising in yellow pages is. These range from our own (very poor) to very good.

Yell.com – My experience with Yell.com is similar to Yellow pages. I do get some quality enquiries through this medium and I believe as the internet evolves this is likely to increase. Yell.com can also be used to link directly to your website.

Ten things to do when marketing a new sign Business

1/ Register a domain name and set up a small website to serve as an online brochure. The site should contain as a minimum contact details and some examples of the type of work you do.

This need not be an expensive exercise. You can put your own site together relatively cheaply and quickly using one of a range of web design software packages available. Even Microsoft Word will allow you to design a website by allowing you to save files as individual .htm web pages. that can be uploaded to a server and used to build a site. Alternatively you may prefer to use a "professional" web designer.

2/ Design and print a number of leaflets

Your normal sign design software will have all of the features you need to design a simple leaflet. When saved as a pdf file this can be sent off to a dedicated print supplier to produce your leaflets for you.

3/ Join your local Chamber of Commerce and/or Federation of Small business. You may then elect to attend the many networking events that are organised. Your business details will also appear free of charge in your local chamber of commerce directory

4/ Place ads in Yellow pages and Yell.com. Link these to your website. Yellow pages only comes out once a year so depending on the time of year you first set up in business, you may have to wait some time before appearing in you local yellow pages. Yell.com is different. You can appear in this almost instantly, and do not forget you have the ability to update your listing at will throughout the year allowing you to promote seasonal offers.

5/ Obtain a mailing list of businesses in your area. You can obtain a list from your local government funded small business advisory centre or obtain a copy of your local chamber of commerce business directory. Go through these lists to determine who your best prospects should be. You can then contact them by mail, email or telephone calls. Even cold calling in person for the prospects you most want to do business with.

6/ Signwrite your van or car and make sure if you are based in commercial premises that you have good quality signs in place

7/ Never forget you are an ambassador for your company. Even when out driving your van, drive with consideration and courtesy. Don't forget other drivers will form an opinion about your business based on your driving manners.

8/ Never forget the best form of advertising is word of mouth. Do a good job for someone and the chances are they will recommend you to some of their friends and associates. Conversely – do a bad job for someone and the chances are they will tell everyone.

9/ Even a job that goes wrong is an opportunity. When a project goes wrong you should view this as a chance to demonstrate your integrity and after sales service.

The first sign I ever did for someone who has since become one of my favourite regular customers went disastrously wrong. When I put my hand up and admitted my mistake and determined to fix the problem my client was suitably impressed and even confided in me that he was more impressed at my attitude towards fixing the problem we had encountered than my overall sales and sign making ability.

10/ Finally – when quiet, don't go offering to do work for silly prices just to keep busy. Your time would be better spent trying to find new customers.

.

Section 15 – Your Premises

Where is the ideal base for you to run your business from?

Well it really depends on your own particular circumstances and the type of work you are planning to do. Are you a one man business or will you be working in partnership with someone or employing others?

Who are your target customers? Is it the business to business sector, or are you targeting the general public?

What types of products and services are you offering?

Home Based

If you are starting on your own then in most cases you will probably elect to work from home. This has the big advantage of no additional overheads. You should however inform your home insurance company that you are going to be running your business from home to ensure you remain adequately insured.

The downsides to being home based are (in many cases) a lack of space. You may also find your neighbours are unhappy at the increased traffic to your home (deliveries and customers). If you live in a flat you may have difficulty getting deliveries upstairs especially large items such as sheet materials.

The other aspect to consider is the effect this has on your customers perception of your company. Particularly larger businesses who may (rightly or wrongly) perceive you as being less professional then someone based in commercial premises. If you are planning to do a lot of vehicle liveries you may also find that weather prevents you from carrying out work on the days agreed with your customers. Customers do not wish to have vehicles off the road for any longer than is strictly necessary and will not be happy to have their work postponed due to wind and rain.

On the other hand working from home can be turned to your advantage in other ways.

Instead of the client having to visit you – you may elect to always go to them to discuss their requirements. In many cases customers may actually prefer it if you will go to their premises to fit their van signs – thus minimising the inconvenience to them. Bear in mind though that this will impact on your own productivity given the need to travel to jobs all the time.

Shop Based

Many prefer to base their business in a retail outlet. This has one major advantage in that being based on a busy main road or high street you will have a much higher profile resulting in plenty of passing trade.

Your shop works as an advert for your business 24 hours a day 7 days a week whether you are open or not. Anyone passing will have an awareness of the type of work you do, and indeed an effective window display and set of display boards should be used to inform any passing trade about the type of work you do. Don't forget what was said earlier:- "It's a numbers game – tell enough people about what you do and you will get the work "

Being shop based has a number of disadvantages:-

1/ Higher overheads. Retail outlets are generally quite expensive in rent and rates

2/ Quality of enquiries. Being high profile will encourage more enquiries but these will not necessarily be quality enquiries. You may be inundated with low value jobs which can be very time consuming simply to deal with – never mind actually producing the work.

3/ Lack of interior space – A shop is unlikely to have a facility to bring vehicles indoors to work on. And the amount of workspace may well be quite limited.

Small Industrial Unit

My personal preference is to base this type of business in a small industrial unit. A one man operation may be able to run successfully from a 500sq ft workshop. Whereas a two or three man business would probably be better suited to a unit size of between 1000 and 2000 sq. ft.

In comparison to a shop – rents on industrial units are much lower. Likewise, rates are also much lower for the equivalent size of premises.

Industrial units will provide you with enough space to bring a range of vehicles from small to fairly large vans indoors to be worked on (something that you couldn't do if home or shop based). The additional space also allows you to build a larger workbench to work on signs, along with increased storage space for materials and equipment.

Though not as high profile as a high street shop – being in an industrial unit nevertheless will provide you with some degree of "passing trade" particularly if you are in a fairly busy industrial estate with a large range of businesses. You will also be seen as having more credibility (rightly or wrongly) than someone who is home based.

The downside is the increased overheads that being based in a unit will cause you. In my experience, one person working on their own will probably struggle to run a viable business from an industrial unit. The increased overheads (over a home based business) will swallow much of the profit that one person working alone is able to generate. However, the sums quickly work in your favour if the business has a minimum of two people working together.

Summary

Home based –

Pros - no overheads

Cons - lack of space, low profile, credibility

Shop Based

Pros - High Profile, high credibility

Cons - High overheads, minimal workshop space

Industrial Unit

Pros - Medium Profile, High credibility, maximium workshop space, undercover work space for vehicles

Cons – Medium Overheads

Section 16 – The internet and its impact on sign making

When we first established our sign making enterprise in 1996 the internet was still relatively unused by the majority of small businesses. However, very quickly the internet "buzz" took off and I still remember people saying in the late 1990's that if you didn't have an internet presence you would not remain in business. How wrong they were!

For any small business to survive it is not necessary to be on the internet….. but without a doubt… it does help!

I never realised at first how much the internet could offer our chosen trade…

Email

The biggest single benefit is the use of email. Nowadays I can speak to a client in the morning, email them a design in the afternoon and have a reply back that evening. When we first started I used to print out my designs and post them to my clients. Email also means my clients can send me their own artwork (examples of logos etc.) for inclusion in our designs. This speeds up the entire design/approval process. It also saves us time and money on postage costs.

Email is also a very useful advertising tool (as explained earlier in the section on marketing). Once you have established a database of customers and/or prospects it is very easy to contact them all with a single bulk email. This is obviously useful for informing customers when you are closed for public holidays etc. But most importantly, it is a means of regularly keeping in contact and reminding as many people as possible about your products and services.

Websites

Most companies now have their own website to promote their business. While it is undoubtedly true to say you can set up and run a purely online business I would never feel completely at ease trusting this as my sole means of selling. What happens if your service provider goes under? Your website disappears along with all your potential customers! However, I do believe now that a small website is an essential part of any small businesses marketing effort.

Our own website is predominantly used to promote the business to customers in our locality. We use Yell.com for this. The website also features on our vehicles (van and car) as well as all paperwork (invoices, letterheads, business cards etc.). In my experience many new customers prefer to browse the website to get an idea of the work we do before approaching us for a quotation for work. We have also made a number of sales directly through the site.

Forums

There are now a huge range of internet forums catering for interests of all types. In the sign making world there are a number of websites with discussion forums that allow the exchange of information between like minded individuals. My own particular favourite is www.uksignboards.com a site set up and run by Rob Lambie who along with his Father runs a very successful sign company in central Scotland. This site also is the focus of the buying group "uksigngroup" formed by Rob Lambie. This buying group allows all of its members to obtain discounted prices on raw materials and sign making equipment and software. Membership of this group is highly recommended.

The internet is also a wealth of information for the signmaker. A couple of my favourite sign utility websites are:-

1/ www.whatthefont.com

This site allows you to upload a scanned image of a sample of writing and will quickly identify any font for you. Signmakers are often given examples of lettering styles to reproduce and often the client will not know the name of the font being used. This site can save you hours of ploughing through font libaries trying to get a font match.

2/ www.brandsoftheworld.com

This site is a massive database of logos used by many manufacturers. Simply type in the name of the brand you are looking for and the database returns a list of options. You can then download an .eps version (vector drawn) of the logo you are looking for.

Section 17 – Your Business Plan

The fundamental question is:- Why do you need to produce a business plan?

The main and most important reason is for yourself.

Of course you will also need to be able to produce a business plan if you need to obtain any funding for your business. Most banks will expect to see your plan before granting any loans and in some cases before even allowing you to open up a business account.

If you are going to be leasing a property to run your business from you will probably also be expected to give your landlord a copy.

Why do you need to spend all that time putting down on paper all the thoughts and ideas that already exist in your head? After all – you are the one with the plan – and that plan was formulated by you in your mind – what advantage is there in laboriously writing it down on paper?

The truth is – no matter how well you think you have thought your business idea through – you will not have foreseen all the possibilities.

Your plan should outline the full scope of your business idea. As you write the plan you will be forced into finding out the answers to a number of questions that are essential for you to make your business a success.

On paper you can describe your ideal scenario – then you can work through the maths to ensure your idea will be viable and profitable. At the end of it all – if you can't convince yourself that this business will be profitable and viable on paper – then what is the point in trying it out for real?

For most people, the hardest (and often most unproven) aspect of the plan is the cashflow forecast. You need this to be able to prove to yourself (and any lenders) that the business is viable and able to return a profit.

When faced with producing a cashflow projection, most peoples reaction is to say "what's the point, it's only guesswork anyway, who knows what will happen in the real world?"

But that's only an excuse for not bothering.

Granted, you do not know in the outset what your turnover will be in the first year, but that doesn't stop you from producing a target. Your target must be achievable (i.e. realistic) and based on hard facts. You should be able to work out the maximum turnover you can achieve under ideal circumstances. Remember there are only so many hours in a day, days in a week, and weeks a year for you to be producing signs. Therefore, your target turnover should be a reflection of these facts and should be a projection of what you can expect to achieve (under ideal circumstances) in your first year or so. Make this your target.

From this you can answer the fundamental question "How much potential profit can I make?" If the answer is none – then there's no point in going any further – you may as well go out and get a job working for someone else.

The simplest way to set up a cashflow forecast is with a spreadsheet. A spreadsheet allows you to play around with different sets of figures to determine their effect on your business.

For example, a properly constructed spreadsheet will allow you to experiment with turnover figures to determine your break even figure. This is the amount of turnover you will be required to make in a year to ensure your business does not run at a loss.

I have produced my own spreadsheet which is a typical model for the small signmaking business. This is a Microsoft excel file which allows you to enter all the specific information that is relevant to your own particular set of circumstances.

For example , how much you pay out in rent, rates, electricity, advertising, fees, telephones and all the other costs associated with running a business.. The spreadsheet then uses all this information to calculate your monthly cashflow based on the turnover figures you enter.

 Once properly set up, you can play around with different circumstances to determine if your business model is likely to succeed, and if it does, how well it can succeed. It also allows you to test your business model to its limits. Proving to yourself just how likely (or unlikely) you are to become a millionaire with your current set of plans. You can then modify your plans until you get the answers you require or desire.

Apart from your cashflow projections (which should be appended to the back of your business plan), the other important aspects of a plan are detailed as follows :-

(Front Page)
BUSINESS PLAN

Business Name -   Enter your business name here

Partners -   Enter proprietor(s) names

Business Address -   Enter your business address

Outline Business Description -   e.g. "Sign Manufacturer"

Accountants -   Your accountants name and address

Banker -   Your bank account details

Date of Plan -   The date your plan was conceived

Business Description

The Business:-

e.g. "Designing, manufacturing, and installing Signs "

In this section you should present an overview of the type of business you will be running.

You should briefly describe the types of products and services you will be offering. You should also describe the type of premises used by the business, whether this be home based, shop based or from a small industrial unit.

You can also summarise here the expected turnover and profits to be made. If the business has been established for some time describe when the business was first established.

You should also describe who your customers are, (e.g. other small businesses like yourself, large corporations, local council, or the general public etc.).

You should also describe briefly how you will obtain your customers (e.g. through websites, advertising or personal contact or a mixture).

Key Personnel

In this section you should describe the key personnel working in the business beginning with yourself

Name –

Previous Experience

Main Duties in the business

Name 2 – Other people involved in the business, their names, experiences and duties and what they will bring to the business

Name 3 etc.

Products And services

Here you should describe in some detail the products and services offered

e.g.

Signage - Vinyl cut lettering and logos are designed on computer and transferred to any suitable surface once cut from a sheet (or sheets) of vinyl.

All of the design is done on a computer using specialised software. The output from the computer is sent to a vinyl cutter or digital printer.

Complex designs can be realised using a combination of vinyl colours but now with digital printing almost any kind of image can be produced. The predominant computer cut vinyl method is much quicker and more economical than the traditional signwriting method.

All work is held on file (computer hard drive) allowing repeat orders to be carried out quickly, accurately and economically without the need to recreate the layout..

The customer will always get a perfect match when ordering a repeat sign (e.g. van livery - newer purchases and/or repaired vehicles are assured of a perfect match to that originally produced).

Any other products and services offered should also be described here

Customers:-

In this section, you should describe who your customers are

e.g.

Mainly other small business, Retail outlets, Garages, Pubs Clubs, Hotels, Taxis, Factories, Van based businesses, Builders. Local council etc.

Market Size –

In this section you should describe the market size for signs. If trading purely locally you should determine the likely numbers of potential customers in your area, if trading nationally or internationally you need to describe the total market available

Swot Analysis

In this section you should identify and describe your companies Strengths, Weaknesses, Opportunities and Threats. In identifying these, also describe how you aim to overcome the weaknesses and threats described

e.g.

Strengths:-

Large diverse customer base

Relevant skills and talents brought to the business by the proprietors and any employees

If you have premises suitable for vehicle livery and assembling large signs

Repeat business based on recreating existing customers signs

Weaknesses:-

e.g.

For a new start business - unknown by many locally

Lack of premises for vehicle liveries and or large signs

Lack of experience

etc.

Opportunities:-

Describe the opportunities identified in your market segment

e.g.

Mail order opportunities via websites.

Threats:-

Increasing competition due to increasingly lower cost of entering the market

Lower prices as a result

Customers not always loyal - shopping around for lower prices

Competition from internet based sign businesses

etc.

Objectives

Personal Objectives:

Describe your personal objectives and reasons for starting this business

e.g. To be involved in a business that we find satisfying and stimulating to run.

Longer term - Build the business into an asset that can either be sold on as a going concern or passed on to other members of the family

Business Objectives

Describe your business objectives and reasons for starting this business

e.g.

To provide a high quality, competitive sign making service.

Provide secure employment for ourselves and any one else involved in the business.

Continue to produce sufficient profits to maintain a reasonable standard of living and still be able to re-invest in the business

Cashflow Projections

In this section you should append your cashflow projections. These can be produced on a spreadsheet as described at the beginning of this section and printed out.

Usually you should include a target projection (best case) as well as a break even and worst case scenario. The aim being to prove to yourself (and any other interested parties) of the turnover required to remain viable.

I remember when we first started and our accountant reviewed our target sales for my first year. I was somewhat put out to hear his comment "you will be lucky to achieve half that". And in reality he was right. Our first years trading was about half that which I had expected having viewed and researched the idea through rose tinted spectacles. Fortunately for us, our break even point was less than half our target turnover, and we remained in business as a result.

After producing your business plan.

So you've produced your plan and you have started your business so what happens now?

Do you leave the plan in a drawer gathering dust? Of course not. You must use it to monitor your real life performance against your expected performance.

As time goes on you will be constantly involved in re-writing your plan as circumstances change and new opportunities arise.

It also serves to re-invigorate your enthusiasm when times get tough. Reviewing your plan serves to remind you of your original objectives and can help to re-kindle your enthusiasm when things begin to flag after a while..

We have been in business for more than twelve years now. Our current plan is titled Business Plan 14!

Conclusion

As with all industries, sign making is constantly evolving, and I believe the future of sign making lies with digital print technology.

Sign makers have had the use of digital print for many years already. Back when I first became a sign maker the Gerber Edge was already a well established tool for digital printing. However, the Gerber Edge is slow and has high running costs. Allied to this is the limited size of prints the machine can produce. Roland entered the digital print market for sign makers when it introduced the PC60 and PC600 thermal transfer print and cut devices. These machines also used thermal transfer technology (as does the Gerber Edge) to print. The main limitations with these devices was their slow speed (each colour – Cyan, magenta, Yellow and black had to be printed in turn to produce the final output). A full CMYK (Cyan, Magenta, Yellow and Black) print meant the vinyl was returned to its starting point before the next colour was laid down. Very slight registration issues could easily ruin the print. Allied to this was the Roland machines notoriety for head failures. Consequently, due to their high running costs and lack of reliability these machines never really fulfilled their true potential. When Roland eventually released it's Versacamm Inkjet print and cut machine the typical sign shop finally had an affordable device that was reliable and quick with low running costs. Precisely what was needed to revolutionise the sign industry.

Without a doubt – computer cut vinyl has many advantages and will remain in use for the foreseeable future as the predominant method for sign making. However, digital print and cut truly has come of age and now allows the modern sign maker to do so much more at prices which are highly competitive. Many jobs that would previously have been done using multiple vinyl layers can now be digitally printed which significantly speeds up the production process as well as reduces costs.

The skills learned in vinyl signs (vector drawing graphics) are also needed as part of the artillery of skills the digital print user must master. Vector drawn graphics can now be enhanced by using gradient fills to achieve effects that cannot be realised using vinyl alone. Photoshop skills can also be utilised to produce stunning designs that can now be created using digital print. Rendered images such as photographs can now also be placed into the typical sign.

Finally, digital printing for sign makers has been taken to its logical conclusion with the introduction of vehicle wrapping. My own view is that vehicle wrapping is an industry in itself separate from the typical sign maker. Designing a vehicle wrap is very specialised and time consuming. Applying a vehicle wrap is equally as specialised and time consuming – thus the whole concept of wrapping vehicles) if done correctly) is an expensive exercise.

I believe partial wraps and digital print and cut designs are likely to become the mainstay of vehicle graphics. These solutions are much less labour intensive and consequently more affordable than full wraps. A well designed print and cut layout can be just as eye catching as a full wrap but can be executed much more quickly.

Digital printing is in itself a massive learning exercise and as such is beyond the scope of this book.

However, for the moment at least, it is still possible to establish a small sign making business concentrating on computer cut vinyl alone.

Index

A

Accounts · 29, 30
Accounts software · 30
Acrylic · 50, 112
Adobe Illustrator · 24, 46, 55
advertisement · 14, 125
Alex Taylor · 16
Aluminium · 50, 113
application fluids · 69
application paper · 64
application tape · 45, 63, 64, 67, 68, 71, 73, 74, 75, 76, 78, 89
applying vinyl · 7, 16, 24, 67, 73, 102, 103
artwork · 55, 153
Artwork Libraries · 55

B

Banner · 51, 60
Banner vinyl · 60
Basic Equipment · 7, 23
brittle · 50, 103
BSGA · 15
bubbles · 61, 67, 68, 72, 73, 74, 79, 110
Business Objectives · 166
business plan · 8, 157, 159, 168
Business Plan · 8, 157, 168
business to business · 144, 149
Butler Dibond · 113, 115

C

Calendered · 57, 58
cashflow · 157, 158, 159, 167
cast · 57, 58
chamber of commerce · 140, 146
Class 1 reflective · 59
CNC router · 113, 114
Cold calling · 140
competitors · 11, 132, 133, 139
conformable · 58
convert to curves · 113

Corel Draw · 24, 46, 55
Corex · 50
craftsman · 14
customer · 11, 51, 102, 104, 110, 134, 135, 137, 139, 143, 163, 164
cut vinyl · 7, 11, 23, 43, 45, 46, 51, 55, 56, 62, 65, 81, 86, 89, 96, 114, 163, 170, 171

D

design · 7, 8, 10, 15, 16, 23, 24, 32, 43, 44, 45, 46, 55, 76, 81, 82, 83, 84, 86, 87, 96, 102, 103, 104, 105, 107, 112, 113, 114, 115, 121, 123, 127, 128, 129, 135, 136, 144, 146, 153, 163
design fee · 115
Design Skills · 15
design station · 46
desk top publication · 46
Desktop Printer · 24
detergent · 26, 52, 69, 72
dibond · 50, 118
digital printing · 8, 24, 46, 55, 56, 163, 170, 171
Digital Printing · 8, 47, 170
DIY · 16
dongle · 45
dry application · 67, 68, 74

E

email · 55, 104, 130, 143, 146, 153
embossing · 57, 61
Etch vinyl · 60

F

Fax Machine · 29
Federation of small business · 142, 146
fixed costs · 132, 133
Flat cut lettering · 7, 8, 112
Flexisign · 45
Fluorescent · 59, 60
Foam PVC · 49, 50

173

Foamalux · 49
fonts · 126, 127, 128, 129
Forex · 32, 33, 49

G

glue remover · 26

H

hanging rail · 92, 96, 97, 98
HNC · 16
hobby · 11
Home Based · 149
hot air gun · 103
Hot air gun · 26
hourly rate · 103, 132, 133, 134, 135, 136, 137

I

illuminated signs · 8, 50
Industrial Unit · 150, 151
Insurance · 17
internet · 8, 142, 143, 145, 153, 154, 165

L

Leaflets · 143
Limited company · 18, 19, 21
Liveries · 7, 102
LLP · 19
locators · 112, 113, 114, 116, 117, 118, 121
logos · 43, 81, 153, 154, 163

M

Magnetic Sheeting · 51
mark up · 115, 133, 134, 135, 136, 137
Marketing · 8, 16, 139, 140, 146
Mastering Layout · 12, 15, 123
MDF · 33, 41
Mike Brown · 11
Mike Stevens · 8, 12, 15, 123, 124, 125
Mitre Saw · 26

Monomeric · 57

N

natural layout · 123, 124, 125, 128, 129
Negative Space · 124
Networking · 141

O

opal acrylic · 50
Opportunities · 164, 165
Organosol · 58
outdoor durable · 107
overheads · 132, 133, 149, 150, 151

P

Partnership · 18, 19
Paul Hughes · 134
perceived value · 135, 136, 137
perspex · 50
Phosphorescent · 59, 60
Photoshop · 43, 44, 47, 171
pixels · 43, 45
plasticiser · 57
plotter · 45, 59, 62, 105, 114
Polymeric · 57
premises · 17, 102, 147, 149, 150, 161, 164, 165
Premises · 8, 149
pricing · 8, 11, 30, 115, 132, 133, 134, 136, 137
prospects · 141, 144, 146, 153
public liability · 17
PVC · 41, 49, 50, 51, 57, 58, 91, 96, 99

R

rapid air vinyls · 61
rasterised · 43, 44, 45, 46, 107
Reflective · 58, 59
repeat business · 102
resolution · 44
Rob Lambie · 11, 154
Roland Versacamm · 55
router · 45, 113

S

safety signs · 55, 59, 143
Scanner · 24, 55
Shop Based · 150, 151
sign layout · 8, 123
sign pricing guide · 134
Sign Software · 7, 43
Signlab · 24, 45, 46, 55
signmaker · 8, 15, 45, 46, 47, 63, 68, 84, 114, 132, 136, 154, 170, 171
signtrim · 49, 50
small business gateway · 10, 17
Small Business Gateway · 17, 140
software keys · 45
Sole Trader · 18
solvents · 58, 103
spreadsheet · 134, 158, 159, 167
Spreadsheet · 30
stand off locators · 113
Substrate · 25
Substrates · 7, 49, 51
survey · 112

T

Telford College · 16
Thermal Transfer · 107
Threats · 164, 165
training · 16
transfer paper · 45, 106
Transluscent · 58

U

uksigngroup · 154
USB port · 45

V

Vector Drawing · 7, 43
vehicle liveries · 102, 149, 165
vehicle livery · 55, 130, 144, 164
vehicle outline · 55, 102, 103
Vehicle signs · 7, 102
Versacamm · 55, 170
viable · 11, 139, 151, 157, 167
vinyl cutter · 10, 23, 45, 46, 55, 163
vinyl cutting · 16, 55, 56
Vinyl Master Pro · 45

W

warping · 49, 91
website · 134, 142, 143, 145, 146, 153, 154
welding · 85
wet application · 67, 69, 79
workbench · 7, 32, 62, 64, 151

Y

Yell.com · 145, 146, 154
Yellow pages · 145, 146

175

"It's better to have tried and failed – then never to have tried at all"

www.ingramcontent.com/pod-product-compliance
Ingram Content Group UK Ltd.
Pitfield, Milton Keynes, MK11 3LW, UK
UKHW041437180426
11947UKWH00007B/491